52 LIFE LESSONS

I Learned the Stupid Way

Meaty Devotionals for Mature Christians

Joy Nevin Axelson

ILLUMIFY

MEDIA.COM

Published by
Illumify Media Global
www.IllumifyMedia.com
"Let's bring your book to life!"

Paperback ISBN: 978-1-964251-94-3

Cover design by Debbie Lewis

Printed in the United States of America

I dedicate this devotional to my beloved dad, Dr. Paul David Nevin, who taught at Moody Bible Institute in Chicago for thirty-two years. Right before he passed away in 2012, I promised him I would get something of his published. Week 3 about hermeneutics consists primarily of Dad's material.

Thank you, Dad, for encouraging me to become a missionary, for proofreading my poetry, and for letting me use your Z89 word processor. I'll see you on the other side.

CONTENTS

INTRODUCTION

Although I'm over fifty, I don't think of myself as an adult. At least not a very *adulty* adult. *Real* adults make their beds every morning, eat fiber for breakfast, and teach yoga classes. They dress smartly, speak authoritatively, and make you feel like you've been called to the principal's office.

A gap exists between my chronological age and how I feel. I'm what people euphemistically call "seasoned." I've traveled to thirty-three countries, lost a parent and two babies, survived cancer, and watched the Twin Towers collapse.

I've gained wisdom from trials, mistakes, and miracles. Like most people, I end up learning life lessons the hard way—by getting smacked down for my foolishness or beaten down by life.

I recently took a course entitled Write Your Life Lessons. When the class ended, it dawned on me: I hadn't chronicled a single life lesson. So I listed a hundred lessons I'd learned. I emailed my list to the teacher who asked, "Do you have any *stories* to go along with these lessons?" "*Do I have any stories*?!" I replied. Uh . . . yeah.

Christian inventor and businessman R. G. LeTourneau once said that when people asked him how he got such good judgment, he'd reply that it came from his experience. "And where did you get your experience?" they would inquire. "From my bad judgment," he would reply.

Jon Acuff once said, "Scars you refuse to hide can become lighthouses that warn other people who are headed to the same rocks you crashed on." If you're tired of shallow, stale devotionals and would prefer to learn life lessons from someone *else's* errors, this book is for you.

Thank you for being brave enough to choose this practical devotional. Each entry consists of suggested Bible reading, a song, a pithy quote, a true story that illustrates a life lesson, application questions, and an original poem. I also recommend a book for those wishing to delve deeper into specific topics.

Although I've been a Christian since 1978, I've made enough stupid choices to potentially spare you a world of pain. Would you like to avoid 85 percent of relational conflict? Do you need your life ruined by a crisis to appreciate others? Do your worst fears need to be realized for you to trust God more?

Around AD 50, the Apostle Paul sent Timothy to Thessalonica to strengthen Christians in their faith and to keep them from being shaken by trials. I hope this book will do the same for you. As my former pastor, Colin Smith, put it, "Imagine standing next to a hurdle. You can't jump a hurdle from a standing position. You have to take a run at it . . . all progress in the Christian life is made by the momentum of our spiritual health." I pray these weekly devotionals propel you deeper in your relationship with God and others.

PROVIDENCE *God's Mysterious Perspective*

My life is but a weaving between my God and me. I cannot choose the colors He weaveth steadily. Oft' times He weaveth sorrow; and I in foolish pride forget He sees the upper and I the underside.

— Grant Colfax Tullar

READ: Deut. 29:29, Isa. 55:8–9, Rom. 11:33–36

When We Grow Most

My father, a theology professor, was declining in health and suffering in the ER. He motioned me closer to his hospital bed. After five strokes, he sounded weak and raspy. His long-utilized teaching voice had dried up. "Joy . . . when do you think . . . you grow most . . . as a Christian?" he managed to whisper. A large lump welled up in my throat. I couldn't speak. I sucked in my emotions, encouraging my soul to be brave. I finally replied with sadness, "When bad things happen."

As Christian pilgrims, we must often traverse shadowy, seemingly interminable valleys. As we set out on our journey, we were naïve. We hoped against hope God would make our sojourn successful by worldly standards. But life never consists of 100 percent positive experiences. The Lord promises in Psalm 84 to make the "Valley of Weeping" into a place of springs as we wind our way up to Zion.

Buyers Are Liars

As fallible humans, we assume we know best. We send our laundry list of demands to God in prayer. "Keep us healthy and wealthy." "Spare us from suffering." In real estate, agents say, "Buyers are liars," when clients modify their search criteria at the last minute. Similarly, we think we know what we want but change our minds when we get it.

If you've attended church long enough, you've heard the tapestry illustration. Behind the scenes, God is weaving the tapestry of our lives, syncing millions of people and situations with an unseen hand. Stray threads dot the back of the tapestry in clashing colors. Since we cannot see the final product, we begin to doubt that the picture on the tapestry is even good.

My husband and I married in 1996. At age twenty-eight, I got my master's degree and we began "trying." At age thirty, I had our son, Soren. We thought it was easy. We "placed our order" with God, telling him how many kids would be ideal. However, God envisioned an unfathomably superior plan.

I soon got pregnant again and miscarried our second child. Desperate to have a sibling for our son, we ponied up cash, setting our hopes on a fertility clinic. But after looming bills and a second miscarriage, we abandoned our "perfect" dream. "Soren," I said to our three-year-old, "it looks like God only wants us to have *one* child, and we're happy we have you. The doctors said we can't have another baby." But Soren proudly declared, "God's gonna give me a baby *sister*!" Every bedtime for two years he would invariably pray, "And God, please give me a baby sister."

Seasons marched by. In 2008, Soren's longed-for baby sister arrived! Why couldn't God have taken a leaf from *our* playbook instead of allowing the heartbreak of failed pregnancies? While we don't fully understand it, the difficulties we encountered made us appreciate our kids more. Of course, I wish we didn't have to pass through this infertile valley to harvest the golden results. As author Tim Keller put it, "God always gives you what you would have asked for if you knew everything that He knows."

APPLICATION

1. Do you think Christians grow most when they experience trials? Why or why not?
2. List three trials you've endured.
3. List what God taught you and how you've grown as a Christian through difficulties.

FURTHER READING: *Providence* (2021) by John Piper

SONG: "God Is in Control" (1993) by Twila Paris

MY ROCK

My Treasure and all I desire,
Author of all perfect things,
through all my life, You've never failed.
My chalice brims with blessings.
I'll blossom where You've planted me
and spread abroad the hope of peace.
My purpose lying at Your feet;

My God, You mean the world to me.
You guard my future, present, past.
Oh, melt my fickle heart of ice.
But by Your hand of Providence,
the silver cord cannot be sliced.
You shield all I cherish, Lord.
Sweetest sleep drifts down like snow.
You keep watch, so I may rest.
Your Spirit whispers to my soul.

I'm running for the finish line;
eternity is all that counts.
To Zion it transports us still,
Your tapestry of plans and routes.
Stronger than the seething swells
that buffet weakened, weary souls,
my Rock stands firm while tempests rage,
though the clouds be black as coal.

WEEK 2

MATURITY *Lessons from a Sad Strawberry*

The proof of spiritual maturity is not how pure you are but awareness of your impurity.

— Philip Yancey

READ: Eph. 4:11–14, Heb. 5:12–14, James 1:2–5

What's more pathetic than an unripe Christian? I like chocolate and strawberries. Just not together. Before removing its chocolate coating, I thought the strawberry was red and ripe. However, after removing the layer of chocolate, I uncovered an anemic beige disappointment. Likewise, when the façade of outward appearance is removed from some believers, it unmasks their lack of holiness and spiritual maturity.

In French, the words for "ripe" and "mature" are the same. This makes a lot of sense. A great chasm lies between what we *believe* demonstrates spiritual "ripeness" and what actually *does* indicate maturity.

Things we *believe* indicate spiritual maturity:
    Attending church
    Tithing
    Volunteering
    Being married a long time

Having well-behaved kids
Being financially blessed

Things that *actually* indicate spiritual maturity:
Serving without recognition
Secretly donating our time, talent, and treasure
Putting others first
Not caring about others' opinions
Enduring trials without losing faith
Feeling convicted of increasingly smaller sins

While the Bible instructs Christians to meet together regularly, just showing up at church proves nothing about one's spiritual maturity. Likewise, donating to charity with ungodly motives means nothing. Volunteering is publicly praised, but many serve because they crave recognition. Being married a long time takes commitment, but some live as roommates for the sake of their children. Parents with well-behaved children should thank God for them. However, they can't take credit when God works in their children's lives. Some assume the wealthy must be mature believers. Not so.

No, the *second* list indicates spiritual maturity. Serving and donating without acknowledgment implies pure motives. Putting others first and prioritizing God's opinion of us shows moral strength. Patiently trusting God in trials is a hallmark of seasoned believers.

Finally, the holier a person is, the more smaller sins will bother him or her. For example, my dad taught theology at a Bible college. When speaking about honesty, he encouraged students to right their wrongs and apologize for dishonesty. He felt convicted for stealing kumquats on the way to school in California in the 1940s. He could've easily rationalized such a trivial act. His family was poor.

That was the only breakfast he had. However, in 1987 Dad wrote an apology letter to the descendants of that neighbor. They readily forgave him. As we age and approach heaven, the Holy Spirit prepares us for it. The more we clean up "little foxes," or small habitual sins, the more prepared we are to spend eternity with our perfect Father.

APPLICATION

1. Have you ever thought that the first list indicated spiritual maturity? If so, which actions and why?
2. Check your maturity level against the second list. Do these actions characterize your life?
3. Which ones are you best at? Which ones could use some work?

FURTHER READING: *Emotionally Healthy Spirituality: It's Impossible to Be Spiritually Mature, While Remaining Emotionally Immature* (2017) **by Peter Scazzero**

SONG: "I Have Decided" (1982) by Amy Grant

LESSONS FROM A SAD STRAWBERRY

The berry looked so plump and ripe;
its green leaves promised flavor.
Once I removed its chocolate stripes,
I spied its lying nature.
Its outward aspects flung aside,
its ripeness I did question.
When light revealed deceitful lies,
I sidestepped its digestion.
May what you see be what you get.
May our façades be real.
May we mature, and better yet,
may good fruit be revealed.

WEEK 3

HERMENEUTICS *Handling the Word of God Rightly*

The text of the Bible means what God inspired it to mean, not "what it means to me."

— Donald S. Whitney

READ: John 14:26, 2 Tim. 2:15, 2 Pet. 1:20–21

I have a dear friend who believes in the prosperity gospel. He claimed Isaiah 53 teaches that Christians need never be sick because Jesus's death healed us. He cited 3 John 1:2, which says (only in the KJV), "I wish above all things that thou mayest proper and be in health, even as thy soul prospereth."

I quickly recognized that these Bible passages were not in context and did not gel with other biblical truths. Such "proof texts" are verses plucked out of context to support predetermined beliefs. So, I inquired, "What about Paul leaving Trophimus sick at Miletus? What about counseling Timothy to drink wine as a stomach remedy?"

Conversations like this underline the importance of understanding sound Bible interpretation principles, or hermeneutics. English preacher, George Whitefield, said, "If we once get above our Bibles and cease making the written Word of God our sole rule both as to faith and practice—we shall soon lie open to all manner of delusion and be in great danger of making shipwreck of faith and a good conscience." Dad and a colleague, Dr. Phillip Lueck, wrote a six-hundred-page hermeneutics textbook entitled "God's Word in Focus," but it was never published. Here are some excerpts from this book. When seeking to understand a passage, we need to ask ourselves **three key questions in order**.

"What did the Bible text mean THEN?"
We must find out what the passage meant *to its original readers*. For example, for the original readers/hearers of 1 Tim. 2:9, it meant exactly what it says. Women should dress modestly. They shouldn't have braided hair or wear gold, pearls, or costly clothing to church. When trying to understand what the passage meant *then*, consider the genre, or kind of literature. For example, below is a list of genres found in the Bible.

1. **Historical Narrative:** Joshua
2. **Law:** Leviticus
3. **Short Story:** Ruth
4. **Wisdom Literature:** Proverbs
5. **Worship Literature:** Psalms
6. **Love Poetry:** Song of Solomon
7. **Prophecy:** Ezekiel
8. **Gospel:** Matthew
9. **Epistle:** Galatians

Consider the context. This includes not only the chapters before and after the text but the entire Bible. If we encounter a passage that appears to imply we can lose our salvation, we must question that interpretation in light of other passages ensuring security of salvation.

"What does the text mean ALWAYS?"

This involves *transcultural evaluation* and *permanent principles*. A permanent principle is something in Scripture that God calls people to do, believe, be, or avoid, regardless of their location, race, culture, or era. Applying God's Word means putting permanent principles to work in our worldview and lifestyle. Going back to 1 Tim. 2:9, God always wants women to dress modestly and not try to flaunt their wealth. This looks different in every culture.

"What does the Bible text mean NOW?"

The final question involves *applying biblical truth*. Danish philosopher, Søren Kierkegaard, considered it his responsibility to *live out* the gospel. He taught that an in-depth understanding of Scripture always transforms the reader.

"God's Word in Focus" lists **four types of applications**:

Conceptual (changing how we think)
Behavioral (changing how we act)
Emotional (changing how we feel)
Testimonial (celebrating what God has done in us)

Here's a sample interpretation using all three questions:

Text: "It is wrong to take a set of millstones . . . as security for a loan, for the owner uses it to make a living" (Deut. 24:6).
Cultural-historical interpretation (THEN): Israelites weren't to take millstones as collateral for loans.
Permanent principle (ALWAYS): God wants us to treat the poor compassionately.

Contemporary application (NOW): If I loan my neighbor $1,000, I shouldn't take his only car as collateral since it's his sole means of transportation. I should either forgo taking collateral or accept something less needed as collateral.

In Dad's retirement speech, he said, "I'm totally sold on inductive approaches to Bible study. It's nice to admire other people's treasures, but it's positively elating to dig and discover gold for oneself! My students have generally responded with enthusiasm and satisfaction to my Bible study methods, though there were always a few who went away sorrowful because they were unwilling to do the hard work of mining their own treasures."

APPLICATION

1. Have you ever learned hermeneutical principles? How can they influence your study of the Bible?
2. Select a passage to interpret. Ask yourself what it meant **then**, what it means **always**, and what it means **now**.
3. Make a plan to pass these principles along to someone who could benefit from them this week.

FURTHER READING: *How to Study the Bible* (2009) by John MacArthur

SONG: "Word of God Speak" (2003) by MercyMe

WE HOLD OUR BIBLES OVERHEAD
(an original hymn)

We hold our Bibles overhead,
standing firm as waves crash down.
By Christ alone our lives are led.
We'll take our stand on solid ground.

CHORUS
God is God and we are not.
We'll not worship self or crown.
Restore the ways the world forgot.
We cannot cave, we won't bow down.

Grace and truth in Christ are wed,
loving others as ourselves.
We'll pull each person from the ledge,
and turn them from the gates of Hell.

Love the sinner, love the saint,
knowing grace cannot be earned.
See others as His fingerprints;
hold true, but with compassion burn.

WEEK 4

VULNERABILITY *Weakness as Strength*

Sometimes God does allow us to crack.... Not because he doesn't love us, but rather to show us and the world his love through us.... when there is light in a perfect jar it is dimmed. But once cracked, the light shines through even brighter. When we allow our cracks and weaknesses to be used for his glory, the light of the gospel can shine through us and his treasure can be seen in us even more.

— Cynthia Holmes-Landry

READ: Isa. 40:28–31, 2 Cor. 12:9–10, Ps. 103:13–14

There's no love without trust. And no trust without honestly sharing our fears, weaknesses, and struggles. It's precisely those chinks in the armor, those tender moments of vulnerability that bind us together. In the four decades I've followed Christ, I've heard many tales of strength shown in frailty.

Even Billy Graham

Evangelist Billy Graham led thousands to the Lord. One day, crowds packed a stadium anticipating a passionate address. Graham approached the microphone. Due to laryngitis, he could barely whisper. The crowd leaned in, paying close attention to every word. Ironically, history records that more people than usual came to

Christ that day. In spite of the abridged, quiet sermon. God's power is perfected in weaknesses. When we face challenges only God can overcome, He gets the glory—not us.

The White Giraffe

My former youth pastor, Rich Tuttle, has taken many mission trips to Ghana. There, they have dubbed him "The White Giraffe." At six foot four, he towers above those he serves. When seeking to share Christ in a new place, Rich secures permission to speak to the village chief.

Once, Rich was rushing to leave for Ghana. At fifty-five, he usually dyed his graying hair brown. However, lacking the time, he flew to Ghana for the first time with his "crown of glory" showing. Rich approached a new village to share the gospel. The chief, a wise old man, listened to what he said. Rich later discovered that the only reason the chief was willing to listen to the "White Giraffe" was due to his white hair. He never dyed it again.

The Art of Kintsugi

Renowned author Joni Eareckson Tada is all too acquainted with hardship. She penned a fascinating article on the Japanese art of kintsugi. It involves gluing pieces of broken porcelain back together with gold glue. Often, the repaired piece ends up being more beautiful than the original.

Decades ago, my mom decorated a vase with paintings illustrating her life growing up on a farm. When she relocated in 2008, movers broke her beloved keepsake. For her birthday, my daughter and I pieced it back together, securing it with golden glue. Inside, we placed a candle. It's so beautiful to see light emanating through the cracked vase. It provides a stunning picture of the treasure we hold in jars of clay. If we try to keep up an "I've got it together" façade, stress rears its ugly head. Isn't it better to allow God to shine hope through our kintsugi cracks?

APPLICATION

1. When have you seen God work mightily through or in spite of weakness or flaws?
2. List three Bible characters who God used in spite of their shortcomings.
3. Contrary to popular belief, God *does* give us more than we can handle. However, He never gives us more than *He* can handle. What overwhelming issue do you need to give to God today?

FURTHER READING: *Anatomy of the Soul: Surprising Connections Between Neuroscience and Spiritual Practices* **(2010) by Curt Thompson**

SONG: "Yet Not I but Through Christ in Me" (2018) by CityAlight

KINTSUGI

Shattered.
like a porcelain vase
along fault lines of weakness

Broken.
lacking utility
helpless to heal heartache

The Artist.
with melted liquid gold
reintegrates my scattered shards

Fractured.
warm waxy candles burning
deep in this heart of fragile clay

Complete.
more lovely now
for through my golden fissures
the Artist's compassion glows

DANGER *The Safest Place on Earth*

We are immortal until our work on earth is done.

— George Whitefield

READ: Ps. 68:20, Pr. 3:23–26, Matt. 10:28

Pastor Colin Smith once preached a thought-provoking sermon. He maintained that the safest place to be is wherever God wants you. He quoted English preacher, George Whitefield, who said we're indestructible until God deems our work on Earth complete. A decade later, I discovered it can be riskier to stay home without God's guidance than to go somewhere dangerous with His blessing.

Don't Die, Mom

Two Filipino friends were planning to return to the southern Philippines on a medical mission in late 2019. Ron asked me to consider joining them. His encouraging smile conveyed a sense of calm purpose. Soon, I accepted this mission. Before our departure, Ron informed me of various hazards we might encounter. My teenage son learned of these and was distraught. "Don't die, Mom," he croaked, wrapping his lanky arms around my shoulders, dragging me down like an anchor.

A Dangerous Oasis

We visited a child sponsorship site in Manila first. There, vulnerable kids are sponsored by Americans. Navigating the path leading to the Gift of Love Center, we pulled our T-shirts up to mask the stench. We understood why these kids, trapped in a cycle of poverty, needed a safe place to go. Later, I discovered that I had risked my safety visiting these cherubic children. Kids often pelted them with stones for attending a Christian center. This haven had been burned to the ground more than once.

The perils described were real. At the Manila airport, heading south, a Filipino man asked, "Miss, is someone picking you up in Zamboanga? It isn't a tourist destination." I reassured him, and we were off, speeding toward the Sulu Sea and the water border with Malaysia.

Where He Leads

Martial law had been declared. In Zamboanga, a peek out of my hotel curtains revealed soldiers carrying guns as tall as themselves. A polio outbreak and widespread malaria threatened our health. A spate of kidnappings had shut down international business there. ISIS had recently abducted three Chinese businessmen and an American. Our team hired Carlo, an off-duty police officer, to guard us as we rode to the most dangerous place we would ever tour—a church.

Zamboanga is on the ocean, so the one-room Protestant church sits on stilts. The "bridge" leading to the church consisted of four bamboo poles loosely joined above the water. Carlo helped us shuffle along the rickety conveyance. Once, my pant leg got caught. I pictured myself plunging, like a circus hippo off a tightrope, into the embarrassment below. Thankfully, I made it safely to the church entrance. "We could pay for a more permanent bridge," we told the pastor. "Oh no," he replied. "When radicals yelling death threats chase us, we pull up this drawbridge so they cannot harm us."

This brave pastor used to be a Muslim cleric. Fatwas had been issued calling for his expeditious murder. *How can someone live and minister amid constant danger?* I wondered. Perhaps the pastor knew what became seared into my consciousness during this hazardous voyage. As Corrie ten Boom said, "Being in the center of His will is our only safety."

APPLICATION

1. What would you think if God was leading you somewhere dangerous?
2. List characters in the Bible who faced danger for Christ.
3. On a scale from one to ten, how much do you trust God to keep you safe until your work is done? Describe a time when God miraculously kept you or someone you know safe.

FURTHER READING: *The Heavenly Man: The Remarkable True Story of Chinese Christian Brother Yun* **(2002) by Brother Yun**

SONG: **"You've Already Won" (2023) by Shane and Shane**

NO TURNING BACK

NO TURNING BACK

I step into warm water;
Sulu Seas roll through me.
There's no turning back.
There's no turning back.

I'm signing my life away.
Each breath might be my last.
And few go with me.
And few go with me.

"You're no son of mine!" he yells.
I cling only to You.
The world behind me...
The world behind me...

With Christ I am intrepid.
For those who kill the body...
The cross before me...
The cross before me...

Though my rugged path snakes through
many trials, toils and snares,
Still, I will follow.
Still, I will follow.

One day faith will turn to sight;
home on heaven's golden shores.
I have decided
to follow Isa.

WEEK 6

WORSHIP *Clicking the Dial of Devotion*

Whatever controls us is our Lord. The person who seeks power is controlled by power. The person who seeks acceptance is controlled by the people he or she wants to please.
— Rebecca Pippert

READ: Mark 7:6–9, Rom. 1:21–33; 10:2–3

Vatican Opulence

One summer, my family and I visited the Vatican. A drought had forced the closure of all the fountains. In spite of the heat, droves of tourists filled St. Peter's Square. Nature abhors a vacuum, and apparently, so do tourists. We chose not to wait in line to tour the basilica—a monument to the wealth of the Catholic Church. I wondered what Peter, that feisty fisherman, would think of this luxurious cathedral. He might be angry or sad, but I'm pretty sure he wouldn't approve.

Paper tickets in sweaty hands, we waited patiently to visit the Vatican and the famous Sistine Chapel. Tour guides herded flocks of visitors through tapestry-lined halls like cattle. Everywhere I looked, gold adorned crosses, censors, and icons. People oohed and aahed at opulent paintings and sculptures. When we finally arrived at the Sistine Chapel, the tiny chamber was packed with gawkers. I felt overwhelmed by the chaos. The environment was neither serene nor contemplative. Noisy crowds and the cha-ching of cash registers drowned out any attempts at prayer.

Where Is Christ?

When I escaped the stuffy maze, I breathed a sigh of relief. It occurred to me that God was nowhere to be found in all of this. Not *once* did anyone worship or thank God for the beauty or the talented artists He created. Rosary beads invited the devout to honor and pray to Mary. Plaques praised popes, but not one praised Christ.

John Calvin wrote that the human heart is an idol factory. Though we don't carve statues to worship, we revere religious figures, financial security, and power. The devil is happy for us to turn the dial of our devotion *just a couple of small clicks* to the right. This results in us worshipping something close to God that isn't actually Him. It doesn't hurt Satan if we pray to saints or light candles. It doesn't strike a blow to the kingdom of darkness if we admire the pope's wardrobe or Michelangelo's talent. It's a genius strategy on Satan's part. People are led to believe they're in a sacred Christian space—that being there somehow brings them closer to God. But for me, all the Vatican treasures can't hold a candle to the glory of the risen Christ.

APPLICATION

1. What matters most to you? Others' opinions? Financial security? The perfect family? What does the Bible say matters most?

2. How can you align your values with those of Christ this week?

3. Are you superstitious? Do you light candles, pray to saints, or check the horoscope just to cover your bases? Do you believe the pope is infallible? What does God say about this?

FURTHER READING: *Counterfeit Gods: When the Empty Promises of Love, Money and Power Let You Down* (2010) by **Timothy Keller**
SONG: "I Put Away My Idols (1982) by Dion

CLICK THE DIAL OF WORSHIP

Worship art, worship power.
Pray to Allah every hour.
Worship love, worship hate.
Pay some money; pass the plate.
Worship self, worship youth.
Trust in anything but truth.
Worship children, worship pets.
Long for luxury and jets.
Worship icons, worship sex.
Donate time; write big checks.
Worship wine, spring for Scotch.
Pay twelve thousand for your watch.
Worship popes, light some candles.
Pay a fortune for your sandals.
Hide behind a thick façade.
Worship anything but God.

PHYSICAL PAIN *Value Apart from Production*

The problem is that when one does not respect life as inherently valuable, as created in God's image, the ruling ethic for value becomes what a person can do rather than who he or she is.

— Michael Beates

READ: Matt. 10:29–31, Rom. 8:28, 1 Pet. 2:9

Four Days

In March 2025, six weeks of digestive issues landed me in the hospital for four days. Colitis almost forced surgeons to resect my large bowel. I had never spent so long in the hospital.

Six Weeks

Shortly after freeing myself from IV needles, my upper right molar began hurting. My dentist had to extract the cracked tooth on April Fool's Day. But it was no joke. The dentist began removing the unsalvageable tooth. Swimming in pain, I found myself blinded by interrogation lights, squirming in a faded chair. Piece by piece, the dentist cracked off shards of tooth. I filled three prescriptions. I thought that was the end of it. However, the tooth extraction had caused a raging sinus infection. For six weeks, I couldn't sleep, work, or breathe. I missed my anniversary and Easter. Two months slipped through my fingers. All I have to show for them are a few lessons I gleaned, which I'll share with you.

What Must I Do?

As humans, our first response to suffering is to wonder why. Those who believe in God's sovereignty know there's a purpose behind even the most challenging circumstances. I didn't feel worthless even though I was "useless." I found myself on solid ground emotionally. At the end of earning approval and the beginning of understanding unconditional love.

Many Americans believe that to be valuable, we must be *producing* something of worth. When incapacitated, we sometimes feel "less than." However, we know God loves us regardless of what we can do for Him. Just being His child is enough. Who among us would love their child less if they were in a coma, unable to "contribute to society"?

Shelton Taguma of Forgotten Voices recently shared a thought-provoking illustration about people's inherent worth. "I have a hundred-dollar bill," he said. "Who wants it?" Everyone's hands shot up. Then he crumpled up the bill. "Is it still valuable?" he asked. Heads nodded. Then he stepped on it. "Is it still valuable? Why?" Although it had been through trauma, its value is determined by its creator. It's the same with us and our Creator. Our God loves bringing beauty from ashes. He's in the business of redemption.

Opportunities

Through physical pain, I've learned that when God places me in a vulnerable position, it provides an opportunity for those who love me to demonstrate it. For example, I pulled the car over to vomit profusely on the way back from picking up my daughter in March.

While I was in a drugstore bathroom cleaning up, my daughter bought me a get-well card with her own money. My pain afforded her a unique opportunity to show how much she loves me. If we never needed help from anyone, how would we know they cared?

Isn't it typical of the God we serve to use our weakness to strengthen relationships and deepen our understanding of His infinite love? Romans 8:28 only applies to believers, but what a balm to realize that God never wastes one speck of our pain.

APPLICATION

1. What are some painful experiences God has used for your good? With whom could you share this testimony this week?
2. Some people believe good Christians shouldn't have to suffer. What Bible characters or verses come to mind to combat this wishful thinking?
3. How can you show unconditional love to someone who's suffering this week? What would God want you to text or write to them to encourage them in their pain?

FURTHER READING: *Hope When It Hurts* (20217) **by Kristen Wetherell and Sarah Walton**

SONG: "Good Good Father" (2016) by Chris Tomlin

WASTING ANOTHER WEEK

What's the point?
Tissues pile high
beside my crumpled bed.
What am I accomplishing?
Empty Afrin bottles litter floors.
March and April have been sucked into a vortex.
Toilet paper rolls, saline solution, prescriptions . . .
When will I be able to breathe again?

When I learn that I am loved no matter what.

WEEK 8

WHAT IF WE WERE THERE? *A Fresh Perspective*

They didn't understand, but that wasn't a reason to leave. They set a good example of faith and patience for us today. The disciples eventually learned what Jesus was talking about. The people who left him, however, remained in ignorance. Although the human desire is to understand everything right away, we need patience when dealing with the teachings of Jesus Christ.

— Michael Morrison

READ: Luke 24:13–35, John 12:16; 13:1–17; 16:17–18

I recently saw a video of Ethiopians watching *The Jesus Film* for the first time in their native language. The gospel story was completely new to them. As Christ hung on the cross, women wept and children cried out. *They didn't know how the story ends.*

I've watched every episode of *The Chosen*. Some Christians complain that characters and storylines are added. This is true. There's a disclaimer in the beginning informing viewers that artistic license was taken to produce a full, detailed picture.

Living the Story

An early episode featured the woman with the issue of blood. We all know the story. After she experienced hemorrhaging for twelve years, Jesus healed her. But *The Chosen* episode brought this story to life for me. It helped me understand the cultural context. Since she was always ceremonially unclean, this poor woman had to live ostracized from others. For an unclean woman to touch this great Rabbi defiled him. Amid dusty throngs of followers, catching a glimpse of the Great Physician was not guaranteed. It took a huge amount of courage and faith for her to risk everything on the chance that Jesus would acknowledge her.

It astonishes me how the producers maintain suspense. Viewers have half the lines memorized since they're direct quotes from the Bible. Spoiler alert: When Christ washes the disciples' feet, they're horrified. This makes sense because this degrading job fell to lowly servants. Peter's visibly upset and confused. He finds a second bowl and jug. As I might do, he tells Jesus that it's *his* turn to wash feet.

You'd Wonder Too

During the last week of Christ's life, the disciples have far more questions than answers. As would all of us in their place. *They don't know how the story ends.* They've heard scores of cryptic parables and confusing promises about the temple, the Kingdom, and death. They're afraid they've wasted three years of their lives. Judas hopes the Messiah will overthrow Rome.

Christ's words and actions only began making sense to the disciples *after* the resurrection. While the disciples had the privilege of spending time with Christ in person, *we* have the gift of the entire biblical canon. *The Chosen* series brought the Gospel accounts to life for me. Now the disciples' bewilderment makes more sense. What if we were there?

APPLICATION

1. How would you react if your Rabbi told you He was ushering in a new Kingdom and then said you were going to fall away after His death?
2. List three seemingly illogical Christian teachings such as, "To find your life, you must lose it."
3. A good understanding of the geographical, historical, and cultural context is key to correctly interpreting the Bible. Choose a passage and research these details. For example, learn which stones were on an ephod or how long it took to walk from Jerusalem to Bethany.

FURTHER READING: *The Jesus I Never Knew* (1995) by **Philip Yancey**

SONG: "Could He Be the Messiah?" (1983) by Michael W. Smith

WHAT NOW?

He spoke in riddles, slept through storms.
He warned us He would come to harm.
Our hopes for kingdoms were erased,
but were these three long years a waste?
So we must now rethink our lives.
We saw the grave site sealed up tight.
How *will* this trying journey end,
when we have lost our dearest Friend?
His body broken, lowered down,
embalmed and left there in the ground.
He said he'd bring His kingdom here,
in victory, banish doubt and fear.
The love that lingered in His gaze
has vanished now, these last three days.
We feel so lost and so alone.
It seems the wicked won,
our hearts so heavy, ripped to shreds,
our tearstained cheeks, our downturned heads.
We have no boats, no nets to mend.
We've left our mothers, brothers, friends.
But such a loss! Such strange events!
The graves disturbed, the curtain rent.
How will this puzzling mystery end?
When will our Rabbi's reign begin?
We can't believe what He's allowed.
We thought we'd live like princes now,
be reigning with the Son of Man.
Our minds just cannot grasp His plan.
Grief hovers, thick, it's such a shock,

but then, we heard our Mary knock.

WEEK 9

GRIEF *Processing Sorrow in Godly Ways*

The difference between what I think life should be and the reality of how my life is equals grief.

— Curt Thompson

READ: Ps. 34:17–18, John 11:1–44, 1 Thess. 4:13–17

Grief Isn't Linear

People talk about stages of grief, but in my experience, grief isn't linear. My dad was declining for three years before he died. Little by little, he lost everything that brought him joy. An avid walker, he broke his femur, landing him in a wheelchair. A connoisseur of fine food, Dad's meals were pureed to prevent choking. Dad loved to teach and sing hymns. Multiple strokes reduced his voice to a raspy whisper. Conversation was a joke anyway since he couldn't hear. Dad loved reading so much he added a library wing to our house. A stickler for order, Dad "Dewey decimalized" all four thousand books. Eventually, he could no longer read at all.

Pre-grieving

When loved ones slowly slip away from us, we experience much of our grief before they leave. We feel sad since they'll never be the same. Grief paralyzes some people. They can't handle visiting those who don't recognize them. They break down sobbing at the sight of their diminished loved one. Others take action. We know we can't "fix" the situation, but we try our best to enrich the person's life while we can.

Dad usually recognized me, but not always. Originally from California, he adored blackberries. In Chicago, the only way to get blackberry pie is to make one. I decided to make one from scratch for him. Proudly, I strode into his room with my prize pie. Dad's eyes lit up, and he gobbled down my offering. "Thanks, Jill!" he said, even though my name is Joy. *Well*, I thought, *at least Dad knows* Jill *loves him and she makes a mean blackberry pie*.

Bring Him Home

Dad knew he would spend eternity in heaven. Not because he had earned it but because he had been forgiven. After three bitter years of suffering, we begged God to take him home to heaven. There, he could embrace his mother and find out who actually wrote the book of Hebrews. He could enjoy luscious fruit.

In 2012, we felt a weight lift when he drifted off in a haze of morphine and woke up with Christ. Later, my friend's father came to live with her family. A retired pastor, he reminded me of Dad so much that I couldn't see him without crying. Dad was gone. No more homemade bread or poetry edits. No grandpa for my babies. Though I needed him, his place at the table sat empty.

The Bottom Line

Dr. Curt Thompson describes John 11 as a one-chapter recap of the entire biblical narrative. 1) God comes. 2) Something goes wrong. 3) Jesus waits. 4) We get mad at God for waiting. 5) God tries to get into the doorway of our grief. 7) We have spiritual debates. 6) Jesus calls for our grief.

Throughout this journey, I learned that grief crops up, uninvited, reminding us of loss. It's okay to sit with that. To tell stories about the deceased and laugh at their quirky habits. Though such discussions are tinged with sorrow, they nourish the soul.

I don't have to keep Dad's memory alive, as though that were all that remained of him. He's in God's presence, and he's more alive than ever. While I wish he were here to offer advice and play with my kids, I know without a doubt I'll spend eternity with him in paradise. And that makes all the difference.

APPLICATION

1. Reread John 11 and match the parts of the story with the overarching biblical story.
2. What loss in life has hit you the hardest?
3. Cry out to God and tell Him how sad you are about your loss. Write a letter to your deceased loved one explaining what they mean to you. Incorporate a tradition into your life that honors them.

FURTHER READING: *For All Who Grieve: Navigating the Valley of Sorrow and Loss* (2020) by Colin S. Smith

SONG: "I Will Rise" (2008) Chris Tomlin

A POEM FOR DAD'S FUNERAL

The laugh I love is gone now, and breath has ceased to stir,
in the lungs of one I'm waiting to inter.
His shell is all that's left here—the butterfly has flown,
and flitted past death's chasm, to his eternal home.
One instant past the threshold, the pain evaporates.
Flooding down comes with the crowns the love his soul awaits.
The patriarchs he pondered, the missionaries crossed,
all gathered with his mother, along the golden coast.
All aching anguish quenching: The glory's just begun.
A thousand juicy orchards for this California son.

BURNOUT *Jethro's Advice*

One sign that I am violating my own nature in the name of nobility is a condition called burnout. Though usually regarded as the result of trying to give too much, burnout in my experience results from trying to give what I do not possess—the ultimate in giving too little! Burnout is a state of emptiness, to be sure, but it does not result from giving all I have; it merely reveals the nothingness from which I was trying to give in the first place.

— Parker J. Palmer

READ: Exodus 18, Acts 6:1–7, Gal. 6:9

We've all heard of Moses. The basket of reeds, the burning bush, and the exodus. However, few of us know Moses' father-in-law, Jethro. Sometimes referred to as Reuel, Jethro lived in Midian (modern-day Saudi Arabia), where Moses fled after killing the Egyptian. Jethro's daughter, Zipporah, married Moses and bore him two sons. Moses stayed in Midian several years before asking Jethro's permission to take Zipporah and the children to Egypt. This request demonstrated Moses' respect for Jethro.

Exodus 18 recounts Jethro's visit to Moses in the desert. The Egyptian army had drowned in the Red Sea while pursuing the Israelites. Jethro had heard of everything God had done for Moses and Israel.

Jethro's Visit

Moses realized the danger posed to his family by the demands of leadership during difficult times. So he sent his wife and sons back to Jethro's home for a break. When Jethro later visited his son-in-law in the desert, he brought Moses' family along. The Israelites were camped near Mount Sinai, where God would give them his law. More than two months had passed since they fled Egypt.

Moses' Impossible Schedule

While visiting, Jethro noticed that the people relied heavily on Moses to resolve disputes and hear from God. Each day spent adjudicating trivial matters drained Moses further since he was attempting to be the only judge for some two million people. He deserves credit for trying so hard. His heart was in the right place.

Jethro's Advice

In his wisdom, Jethro knew that weighing in on petty disputes wasn't the best use of Moses' time. Instead, Jethro proposed a solution found in modern business administration textbooks: delegation. Jethro noticed that without assistance Moses was getting burnt out by the sheer volume of daily tasks. So, he counseled Moses to choose godly judges to adjudicate smaller matters and to delegate less important tasks to them. This would free up Moses to focus on what God was calling him to prioritize. Of course, Moses had to be humble enough to follow his father-in-law's advice.

Finding Support

Leaders aren't meant to bear their loads alone. They cannot (and should not) feel it is their responsibility to be all things to those they serve. Instead, the church ought to function like a symphony. Each distinctive instrument is necessary to achieve the common goal of playing a piece. Like the servant in Psalm 123, all must watch for the slightest movement of the conductor's hand to carry out his will. While being supported by others, church leaders must focus on playing *their* part.

Focusing on Our Calling

If we're honest, we must admit that there are *very few* things that *only we* can do. Only we can be good parents or spouses to our particular families. Only we can keep ourselves physically or spiritually fit. But most other tasks can be delegated. To avoid burnout, we must follow in Moses' footsteps. Delegation includes giving up the desire to control situations or to do things perfectly. This week, let's focus on what God has uniquely gifted each one of us to accomplish and create margin by delegating the rest.

APPLICATION

1. List at least three jobs that *only you* can do.
2. Are your church leaders burnt out? If so, why? How can you encourage them this week?
3. If married, how well do you get along with your in-laws? It's important to maintain positive relationships. Whom could you get along better with, and where will you start?

FURTHER READING: *Pastor to Pastor: Tackling the Problems of Ministry* (1987) by Erwin Lutzer

SONG: "Praise You in This Storm" (2005) Casting Crowns

DELEGATE!

(My dad, Dr. Paul Nevin, helped create
this lesson and wrote this poem to accompany it.)

If you find yourself in charge, delegate! Delegate!
If your job is much too large, delegate! Delegate!
If the work is never done, delegate! Delegate!
So you'll have some time for fun, delegate! Delegate!
If you face the burnout threat, delegate! Delegate!
This resolve you'll ne'er regret, delegate! Delegate!
Choose the worthiest ones in fact; delegate! Delegate!
Trust them with the power to act; delegate! Delegate!
They can take the simpler cases; delegate! Delegate!
Harder ones the chief embraces; delegate! Delegate!
This will spare you much fatigue; delegate! Delegate!
Save you time you really need; delegate! Delegate!
Slow the strain that makes you ill; delegate! Delegate!
Lengthen life and joy fulfill; delegate! Delegate!

WEEK 11

SPIRITUAL BALANCE *Intellectual vs. Emotional Spirituality*

True worship is balanced and involves the mind, the emotions, and the will. It must be intelligent; it must reach deep within and be motivated by love; and it must lead to obedient actions that glorify God.

— Warren Wiersbe

READ: Ps. 95:1–7, Mark 12:28–34, 1 Cor. 14:26–32

Where's the happy medium between knowing *about* God and experiencing the rush of the Holy Spirit? Is it possible to love God with your mind *and* experience His power and inspiration? After five decades of worshipping in twenty countries, I've yet to locate this white whale of biblical balance.

The Intellectual Approach

I grew up in a conservative church where sermons sounded like seminary classes—intellectually stimulating but devoid of emotion. In many conservative churches, congregants knowingly smile at each other with each mention of advanced terms like Ebenezer, Nazarite vows, or phylacteries. People show up on time. Library lighting beams down on the stark pews. In some settings, Christians feel like freaks if they raise their hands, clap, or say a peep during worship services. As a Caucasian conservative, I've been programmed to avoid embarrassing myself or others during church. I can't show too much emotion or move . . . not even an inch.

However, our doctrine has always been on point. We knew Romans Road and could debate tribulation viewpoints. We memorized Bible verses and had assurance of salvation. Puffed up with head knowledge, we memorized Greek words and tenses, chiming in with extrabiblical information.

We knew much *about* God but often had to admit we had little experience *of* God. We failed to listen for His voice. We tended to err on the side of cessationalism "just in case." Our intellectual curiosity was satisfied, but our heart cries frequently remained unheard. Our burdens unshared. Our closeness with God unrealized.

The Experiential Approach

At Pentecostal-leaning churches, self-expression is the order of the day. To demonstrate spiritual connection, congregants wave their hands like they're at a rock concert. Some speak in unintelligible tongues without interpretation. "Amens" and "hallelujahs" echo through smoke and colored spotlights. Pastors provide few insights of substance. Instead, the focus is on powerful emotional experiences.

One summer in Paris, at the pinnacle of Montmartre in the shade of Sacré-Cœur's white dome, I heard Christians singing. Curious, I struck up a conversation. One lady asked if I'd been baptized with the Holy Spirit. "Yes," I replied. "I became a Christian at age five and received the Holy Spirit at that time." Shaking her head, she told me I needed a *second* baptism of the Holy Spirit. And to prove it, I had to speak in tongues.

A Happy Medium

I propose that Christians would be better off adopting *neither* of these extreme examples. Why not make it comfortable for people to worship God in meaningful ways, like kneeling, crying, or "raising holy hands"? Why not stick like glue to sound doctrine instead of focusing on entertainment or emotional reactions? Why not insist that if people speak in tongues we follow Pauline instructions and provide interpretation?

We *must* strike a balance, finding ways to connect emotionally with the God of the universe while sticking to the doctrinal straight and narrow. Expecting God to do miracles but not treating him like a cosmic vending machine. Focusing on all three Persons of the Trinity instead of just one.

APPLICATION

1. Which side of the emotional/intellectual spectrum does your church fall on? What could be done to achieve a more balanced, biblical approach to worship?
2. How can we help intellectual Christians experience God more?
3. How can we prioritize biblical truth over emotional experiences in our Christian walk?

FURTHER READING: *Keep in Step with the Spirit: Finding Fullness in Our Walk with God* (2005) by J. I. Packer

SONG: "Heart of Worship" (2019) by Matt Redman

TRUE WORSHIP

True worship is a weapon,
turning worried thoughts to God.
We raise our hands to heaven,
seeking comfort from beyond.
The Holy Spirit's presence
rushes through this sacred space.
Our minds are fixed on knowing Him,
our motives fixed on grace.
The dial can shift from head to heart
or lean toward rigid facts.
But all believers realize
beliefs are proved by acts.
We rightly handle God's commands;
we learn the ways He moves.
And so we bow on bended knee
to serve the ones He loves.
We worship God with heart, soul, strength,
and mind to be complete.
In heaven, we won't just observe.
We'll worship at Christ's feet.

WEEK 12

GENDER DYSPHORIA *Truth and Love*

Loving a person means telling them the truth when their lifestyle and thinking are detrimental to their health.

— Brandon Sutton

READ: Deut. 22:5, Rom. 1:24–27, Eph. 4:14–15

"Mom, I'm trans." Our daughter upended our world with those words in 2021. After transitioning from Christian school to public, she faced bullying for her faith and for her weight. So she began to identify as a trans male, choosing a new name and pronouns. Hers was a case of Rapid Onset Gender Dysphoria (ROGD) since she never acted masculine.

The good news is that Christians don't have to choose between affirming an unbiblical worldview and hating the LGBTQ community. We need to interact with others in ways that are both truthful and loving. God endorses neither loveless truth (hitting non-Christians over the head with verses) nor truthless love (endorsing sin out of compassion).

Transgender ideology operates like a cult, urging dysphoric kids to disconnect from families who don't affirm the lie, labeling dissenters as "transphobic." It redefines "love" to mean agreement and "support" as compliance with demands. These could include puberty blockers, cross-sex hormones, or irreversible surgeries.

According to these definitions, we don't love *or* support our daughter since we're not ready to throw our faith out the window. Below are five lessons my husband and I learned the hard way.

Choose Your Battles

Although it may seem loving, never affirm gender dysphoria. Choose your battles carefully. Let cosmetic issues, like hair length, slide. We drew the line at pronouns. Using male pronouns for our daughter felt like agreeing with an anorexic that they're overweight. Truth must anchor our faith. Pretending that switching genders is the solution is unbiblical. When it comes to gray areas, we must make decisions with a pastor's advice and an open Bible.

Maintain Strong Relationships

Kids listen to those they feel love them most. This *has* to be you, *not* the trans community. Children aren't the enemy. They're victims of this harmful lie. Discover each child's love language and speak it daily. Resist the temptation to resent them for the crisis they caused. As Barbara Johnson said, "Never let a problem to be solved become more important than a person to be loved."

Garner Support

In the liberal area where we live, we constantly swim upstream. As Romans 1:25 says, our culture has "traded the truth about God for a lie." Not "affirming" our child is the hardest thing we've ever done. But we don't have to walk this road alone. When our journey began, we consulted our pastor and a Christian counselor, enlisting their help as we navigated these uncharted waters. To keep transgender propaganda from infiltrating impressionable minds, ensure your child's doctors, teachers, and counselors share your values.

Pull the Plug

Shelter kids from harmful influences like internet chat rooms like Discord, videos by trans influencers documenting medicalization, "woke" TV shows, and people celebrating dysphoria. Giving a dysphoric child access to the internet is like sending an alcoholic into a bar. Boost cybersecurity and only allow "dumb" phones without internet access.

If possible, send kids to a Christian school or consider homeschooling. I cannot emphasize enough that everyone influencing kids struggling with gender issues *must* be grounded in the truth. If not, false teaching could lure them away.

Pray

When you've done all you can, acknowledge that the results are out of your hands. Second Corinthians 3 speaks of blinded minds unable to see the truth. Since only God can change hearts, prayer is our first and last resort in all situations. Thankfully, we serve a God who is mighty to save.

We've been battling this for five years. Early on in this crisis, we resolved not to let Satan have our child. God began a good work in her. We trust Him to complete it. Our daughter has made significant strides toward accepting who God made her to be. For believers, God only writes good stories. So if your story isn't good yet, it isn't finished.

APPLICATION

1. Do you know anyone with gender dysphoria? How can you show this person love without affirming the lie that they were born in the wrong body?
2. Will arguing draw people closer to God? How can you hold up God's beautiful design of two sexes/genders instead of trying to dismantle flawed logic?
3. How can you stand up (lovingly) for the truth about gender identity this week?

FURTHER READING: *Raising Gender-Confident Kids: Helping Kids Embrace Their God-Given* **Design (2025) by Kathy Koch and Jeff Myers**

SONG: "You Say" (2018) by Lauren Daigle

THE WOES OF SOWING

Spring arrived; I planted seeds,
among my old ancestral fields.
I labored under wind and rain,
my eyes ablur, my spirit strained.
One year, a sunflower sprouted forth,
the golden sunshine of my youth.
Although it aimed to reach the sun,
it could not end what was begun.
Surprised, one spring, some wildflowers grew,
dainty bells of pink and blue.
I fertilized their barren clay
and sheltered them from winter's rage.
I sprinkled on them tears of love,
but weeds attacked their nascent buds.
The pink blooms were the first to fall.
I feared the fate that would befall
my gentle sprouts, so wracked with needs.
A border made to block the weeds
was quickly set in place to save
my precious petals from their grave.
Each dawn and dusk, I linger still,
and I compassionately till
the clods of earth that stunt their growth.
I battle thorns with nail and tooth.
But many days, intent to die,
I fear my flowers cease to try.
With failing hope, I'm going mad.
All I want *now* is what I had.

REST *Sabbath Practices for Christians*

At the heart of personal well-being is the Hebrew word shalom, *which is most often translated "peace." Shalom is something desirable, which ultimately comes from God. It refers to a deep sense of goodness, safety, wholeness, and well-being. It is this last word—well-being—that best captures the importance of the EFCA's commitment to being before doing.*
— The Evangelical Free Church of America

READ: Mark 2:23–28, Rom. 14:5–6, Heb. 4:9–10

Remember snow days in elementary school? Without even a holiday, we were gifted one day off. On these beloved days, I slept late, watched cartoons, and played outside. Peter Scazzero, in *Emotionally Healthy Spirituality*, reminds us that God gives us one day off *each week,* yet we often neglect to take it.

Our Daily Manna

While we're no longer under Old Testament law and can work when we want, God's model of resting one day out of seven remains ideal. Genesis 2:2–3 says that God blessed the seventh day of Creation and rested from His work. He *created* humans. In our "user manual," He specified that we weren't built to labor 24/7. We require down time each week to relax, refocus, and reboot. Intentionally taking one day off per week involves trusting that the Creator is in control.

Exodus 16 recounts how God provided manna to the Israelites. This heavenly bread would spoil if stockpiled overnight . . . with one notable exception. God literally gave them their "daily bread" each morning. They were *only* allowed to save any on the day before the Sabbath to avoid working on their day of rest.

Under Grace

While Sabbath-keeping isn't commanded in the New Testament, resting weekly remains God's best for us. Jesus kept the law perfectly, but even *He* was flexible in his interpretation of "work." The religious leaders had gone overboard, adding extra rules to the law. They grew proud of how perfectly they avoided work on the Sabbath. They considered picking a little grain or dealing with emergencies on the Sabbath sinful. Jesus set them straight. He said God created the Sabbath to *benefit* people, not to *burden* them.

Margins

I estimate that we adults spend 80 percent of our lives doing activities we dislike. "Adulting" involves fulfilling our responsibilities regardless of whether or not we "feel" like it. When each workday provides little renewal, taking days off becomes a mental health necessity. When we don't follow God's rhythms, we feel harried and overwhelmed. We end up ignoring our calling in favor of putting out fires. We fail to prioritize important things like goal setting, praying, and reflecting.

According to Pastor Mark Buchanan, "Most of the things we need to be most fully alive never come in busyness. They grow in rest." Since college, I've found it helpful to take regular retreat days or three-hour breaks to meet with God. I call them TAG times (Time Alone with God). At the start of TAG times, I offload scheduling details, worries, etc. from my brain by filling out my calendar, creating a to-do list, and listing everything I'm worried about . Then I ask God to reveal the "big rocks" on which I should focus during this life season. When we schedule what matters most, the "smaller rocks" neatly fall into place around godly priorities. During retreat times, the idea is to approach God's throne and whisper, "Speak, Lord, for your servant is listening." (1 Sam. 3:9)

Pick a day. It doesn't have to be Sunday. But always keep church time sacred. This may mean no Sunday morning sports, brunches, or open houses. In college, I'd pretend that Saturday was the last day I had to study before Monday. This practice brought me peace. On your day of rest, focus on activities that allow you to relax and enjoy God's good gifts.

Ultimate Rest

Maranatha! We await with anticipation our heavenly home and the reversal of the curse that rendered work unpleasant. In the meantime, let's take advantage of the spiritual rest we have through Jesus. Instead of scrambling to earn grace, let's rely on Christ's declaration, "It is finished!" (John 19:30).

APPLICATION

1. Which day of the week will you protect as your day of rest? How will you ensure you can rest that day?
2. If you're currently "spread too thin," why do you think that is?
3. Schedule a Sabbath retreat. Go to a library, church, or park. Read the Bible and a good Christian nonfiction book. Whenever you sense God speaking, write down what He says. If they're action points, make a to-do list.

FURTHER READING: *Sacred Rhythms: Arranging Our Lives for Spiritual Transformation* (2006) by Ruth Haley Barton

SONG: "Still" (2020) by Rend Collective

STILLED (Psalm 131)

I'm unconcerned with lofty things;
my soul is calm and stilled.
Needing nothing, satisfied,
my turbulence is quelled.
My mind, a glassy, moveless pond
of waters pure and smoothed;
pacific waves roll through my frame,
but *I* cannot be moved.
Provision, like a flooding stream,
goes far above beyond.
Asleep inside His warm embrace,
my furtive fears are calmed.
My muscles lax, no longer tense,
my every nerve at peace,
in quietness and confidence,
my strength shall be increased.

NETWORKING *Miraculous Providence*

Ultimately, kingdom partnerships are not about transactions, but about transformation. . . . It's about what God has given me to share with you so we can complement (complete) one another. This attitude . . . will ensure lasting fruit in your partnership with God and others.

— Arjo de Vroome

READ: Jer. 10:23, Dan. 4:35, Acts 4:27–28

At a Christian conference, the speaker had us turn to those seated nearby and say, "I have needs to be met," and "I have gifts to share." My philosophy of networking is that you don't have to *have* anything or *know* anything. You just have to *know someone* who has it or knows it and connect the dots. The secret to this philosophy is knowing the God of the universe, who controls all things. I learned the joy of sitting back and watching God network. Below are some true stories.

Philippines/India/USA

In 2019, I participated in a mission trip to the Philippines. There, leaders shared that an Indian doctor from my church had anonymously funded surgeries. I'd never heard of him before then. Later that day, I received an urgent message from a Christian in India. His young adult daughter, who lives near me, needed urgent medical attention for life-threatening lupus. However, she had no health insurance.

God brought to mind the doctor in Chicago. I gave her father and the doctor each other's contact information. The daughter received care the next day. The amazing thing is that I had to be in the *Philippines* to learn of this Good Samaritan who attends our church.

Montreal/France/Nashville/Congo

When I was thirty-seven, my parents passed along a newsletter for a charity called Bibles and Literature in French. I visited their office since it was based nearby in a suburb of Chicago. Since I'm a translator, I offered to provide French–English translations as needed. Nine years later, BLF asked me to consider joining the board and I did.

Francis Cabrel is my favorite French singer. He only tours Canada every three to five years. Since he recently turned seventy, I wanted to check seeing him in concert off my bucket list before he kicked the bucket. I got tickets to see him in 2024 in Montreal.

Making the most of this trip, I reached out to the president of BLF Canada, Toe-Blake Roy. He picked me up at the airport. I told him my dad had coauthored a hermeneutics textbook with his colleague, Dr. Lueck. I could almost see the wheels turning in his head. "Why don't we translate it into French for Quebec and Francophone Africa?" he queried. Dad passed away in 2012 without his life's work being published. My mom signed a translation agreement.

Every September, I attend the GlobalFingerprints summit in Minneapolis. I needed to see ninety-year-old Dr. Lueck in person to get the book release signed. He just "happens" to live thirty minutes from Minneapolis. I met with him, and he signed off on publishing the textbook in French.

This tome will likely be printed at the Christian print shop I visited in France in May 2024. Then, textbooks can be sent to a seminary in Kinshasa, Congo to be used by a Congolese hermeneutics professor I met "by chance" at a conference of over 3,000 people in Nashville, TN. I have never met another hermeneutics professor who teaches in French.

Congo/Liberia/USA

While teaching history in Liberia, my brother, Tim, befriended Dr. Lee Newton. Lee's daughter, Olivia Newton, whose nickname is Sweet Tea, had just moved to Iowa for college. Alone in a new country, Sweet Tea was ill-equipped for the impending winter, having never seen snow.

Since I help refugees, Tim called and asked if I could raise funds to purchase her a winter coat. "I can do better than that," I replied. I formulated a plan to ensure that Sweet Tea not only had a coat but substitute parents and cultural information to help her adjust to life in America.

In 2004, I traveled to Congo and met a missionary hero of mine, Dr. Tim Wester. Recently, Dr. Wester and his wife retired to Iowa. God brought this to mind when I learned of Sweet Tea's whereabouts. Shortly after asking Dr. Wester and his wife to reach out to Olivia, they'd taken her out to lunch, bought her winter clothing, and explained many cultural differences. My brother isn't a believer, but he knew Christians could help. Back in Liberia, I'm sure Olivia's dad breathed a sigh of relief knowing his daughter was cared for.

APPLICATION

1. God orchestrated minute details in these networking stories. How does that inspire you to trust God to handle your challenges?
2. Give one or two examples of providential God stories. Share them with someone this week.
3. What excites you about God's powerful and miraculous plan? Let's boast about God and lift Him up this week.

FURTHER READING: *The Case for Miracles: A Journalist Investigates Evidence for the* **Supernatural (2018) by Lee Strobel**

SONG: "Miracles" (2020) by Colton Dixon

HIGH ABOVE

(an original song)
Unfailing love, vast as the heavens,
faithfulness beyond the mist,
all-encompassing, limitless love.
In open hearts, Your work persists.

CHORUS
High above, my God, You're High above
every circumstance that I'm thinking of.
You are mighty, and God, You're in control,
as every detail of my life unfolds.

Righteousness like mighty mountains.
Your justice jets to the ocean floor.
You're unchanging, firm and eternal,
Your mercy crashes from shore to shore.

Unafraid, we're sheltered, safe,
Beneath the shadow of Your wings.
With lavish love, You welcome us,
and our spirits start to sing.

Judgments wise as sea is water,
sparking flames in lightless nights.
You sealed our souls for once, forever.
Lord, we lift Your name up high.

PURPOSE *What God Created Us to Do*

You will be most effective when you use your spiritual gifts and abilities in the area of your heart's desire and in a way that best expresses your personality and experiences. The better the fit, the more successful you will be.

— Rick Warren

READ: John 4:34, Col. 3:23, 1 Pet. 2:9

Optimizing the Second Half

Games are won or lost in the second half. I recently turned fifty. I hope this applies to life. In John 4:34, Jesus explained that His nourishment came from finishing the work prepared specifically for Him to do. Surrounded by pressing needs, Jesus had to intentionally allocate His time.

It's not easy to pinpoint our calling in life and prioritize accordingly. We often hand God our plans, expecting Him to stamp them with His approval. Wouldn't it be nice to discover what God has prepared for us to do with our time, talents, and treasure?

Doing Too Much

At age forty-eight, I was stressed to the gills. I ran a real estate company. I did translating, substitute teaching, and tutoring on the side. Worried about money, I spent most of my time doing jobs I didn't feel called to in order to pay for our children's Christian school tuition.

After turning fifty, my former youth pastor pulled me aside. "Joy, you're doing too much," he said. Holding back tears, I responded, "I know." He assured me that "the hand that guides is the hand that provides." He reminded me that God would enable me to focus on the ministry He created me to do.

Thankfully, I took that leap of faith. I became a part-time missionary using my French degree. I have to raise my meager monthly support, but I'm not stressed. I know I'm right where God wants me. I've begun getting my poetry and devotionals published. Although it doesn't pay well, it's gratifying, and God has richly provided.

Let Them Flow

Perhaps you've heard the question, "If you could attempt anything for God, knowing you wouldn't fail, what would you do?" I've recently turned my focus to making a lasting impact for Christ while I have the chance. One way I do this is by working for a Christian child sponsorship program called GlobalFingerprints. This nonprofit changes lives and eternal destinies.

I now feel like my daily activities work in synergy. My volunteering, parenting, child sponsorship ministry, and even real estate work all smoothly fold together into what God created me uniquely to do. As Francis Havergal wrote, "Take my moments and my days; let them flow in ceaseless praise."

APPLICATION

1. What are your gifts, and what are you passionate about?
2. How can you focus on "what God created you to do" at this point in your life?
3. Ask God to show you what to prioritize. What's one thing you know God wants you to do this year? Write down His response and put it into practice.

FURTHER READING: *Unstuck: Out of Your Cave into Your Call* (2014) Mark Jobe

SONG: "Do Everything" (2011) by Steven Curtis Chapman

THE PIVOT

Nose to the grindstone four decades down,
still selling my soul to the real estate store,
worried and working, stress out of control.
Detesting this phase, sleepwalking through days,
tossing and turning, market downturning,
driving in dark rain, smiling in stark pain.
Longing to live with purpose once more . . .

Beginning to bloom, five decades loom
from seeds planted deep, passion and poetry,
compassion and gifting running free.
Months fast flying by, contentment can't lie,
leaving a legacy, dreaming of destiny,
smiles without trying, finished with crying.
Truly fulfilling my purpose to soar.

UNITY *The Body of Christ*

I believe God made me for a purpose, but He also made me fast. And when I run, I feel His pleasure.

— Eric Liddell

READ: Rom. 12:6–8, 1 Cor. 12:18–21, 1 Pet. 4:10–11

I have an easy question for you. What do they usually serve at men's breakfasts at church? That's right. Bacon, toast, pancakes, sausage, and more bacon. What about at a women's brunch? Spinach and egg white quiche, fruit, and herbal tea. I cannot correct this miscarriage of justice. But I *will* bend stereotypes and share a football analogy.

Da Bears

If you've ever lived near Chicago, you've heard of the legendary Chicago Bears who won the 1986 Super Bowl. If you're a *true* Bears fan, you can sing the words to the ridiculous music video the team created called "The Super Bowl Shuffle." In it, each primary team member sings a verse about their particular position. We all loved Walter Payton, who sang, "They call me Sweetness and I like to dance. We've had the goal since training camp to give Chicago a Super Bowl champ."[1] In contrast to the agile running back, William "The Refrigerator" Perry, an imposing tackle, sang about his defensive role on the team. From the quarterback to the kicker to the wide receiver, each teammate played a specialized role.

Power in Diversity

After watching the Bears win recently, my husband said that, as opposed to football, most baseball players can have the same physique and it doesn't matter. In general, lining up a good baseball team requires no specific body type. In football, however, diversification is key. You need tall receivers, sturdy linemen, and an accurate kicker. Each player has a different skill set, body type, and role. But they all must function as a unified team to win.

This illustrates how the body of Christ works best. According to 1 Corinthians 12, the church consists of many members with different functions. Every Christian has unique spiritual gifts and a special role to play in God's family. Not everyone can be the pastor. Some people need to teach Sunday school. Others play instruments. Still others vacuum floors. All these jobs have equal value in God's sight.

Feeling God's Pleasure

This week, instead of seeking high-profile roles at church, prayerfully ask God to reveal your specific gifting—what makes your eyes light up. Then find a way to serve using your unique abilities and gifts. I love teaching French to American kids. When I went on a mission trip and taught ESL to French-speaking kids, I felt ecstatic. It didn't seem like work to me, because God *made* me to do it. Let's leverage our talents and experience to build up the Church this week.

APPLICATION

1. Make a list of your talents, spiritual gifts, and experiences. Ask God how you can serve the Church with these today.

2. Do you envy high profile gifts, like preaching? Ask God to impress upon you the importance of what *you* were created to do.

3. What types of serving have brought you the most joy? Why?

FURTHER READING: *The Life We're Looking For: Reclaiming Relationship in a* **Technological World (2022) by Andy Crouch**

SONG: "He Reigns" (2003) by Newsboys

EACH ONE COUNTS

I'm not first violin; I'm just timpani.
I'm not the conductor; I don't really count.
The bassoon has few parts. I'm not that important.
I just play the cymbals, but they *are* quite loud.
I'm not the head coach; I'm just a receiver.
I'm special teams and often off field.
All I do is kick. I'm not on the poster.
I blitz their QB; he infrequently yields.
I'm just a gland, but my job is important.
I'm not the brain; I'm just the spleen.
I'm not the right hand, just a pinky toe.
I'm the optic nerve, but I'm never seen.
In the Church universal, each person is needed.
Each person is cherished. Each one plays a part.
Some parts get attention. Some hide in the shadows.
Some hold up the others to shine in the dark.

TAKING OTHERS FOR GRANTED *Falling into Place*

I wish I could still put his socks away.

— A thirty-nine-year-old widow

READ: Prov. 27:1–2, Eccl. 4:8–12, James 4:13–16

My real estate career had taken off. Feeling prideful, I was frequently annoyed. Annoyed that my husband was, in my biased estimation, not pulling his weight at home. In spite of working full-time and participating in family activities, he didn't have perfect record when it came to chores I'd assigned him.

Do I Need Him?

In December 2016, I thought to myself, *What do I really need my husband for anyway? I make enough money on my own, and he's not helpful at home.* In hindsight, that was a *very* foolish thing to think.

Three days later, I was descending our stairs at eleven p.m. Four stairs from the bottom, I slipped and fell, crashing my kneecap down on the hard slate floor! It killed! All I could do was scream. No words escaped my mouth, just an anguished groan. "Aaaahhh!" For a minute, this cry pierced the silence of our dark home. My husband appeared on the landing. "Stop yelling," he said in a calm, authoritative tone. So I switched to shouting, "Call 911! I broke my leg!" I was terrified to look at my leg, certain I'd find a compound fracture with bones jutting out like the steel wreckage of 9/11.

An ambulance rushed me to the ER. Fentanyl reduced my agony to a mere seven out of ten. I had completely severed my patellar tendon, which connects the lower leg to the knee. The next day, I had emergency surgery. The surgeon drilled three holes in my kneecap and reattached the tendon. The inside of my knee required fifteen stitches. Finally, this whole mess was capped off with twenty-eight staples, like mini railroad ties bridging the crest of my knee.

Without Him, I Could Do Nothing

At home, I would crawl upstairs each night and try to block out the pain. I could sleep four hours at a time using a professional ice machine. At three a.m., my husband had to add ice so I could continue sleeping. In my newfound helpless state, I couldn't get to the bathroom or shower by myself. I couldn't cook, walk, or drive. I found myself completely dependent on my "unnecessary" husband. *Very funny, God,* I thought. I had fallen, literally, *so* far from my prideful perch of one week prior.

Lord Willing

Taking my husband for granted wasn't my only sin. I also played God by pretending I knew the future. Every year, I send out a Christmas letter chronicling the main events in our lives. That year, I flouted the commands in James 4 warning Christians not to assume anything about the future. I'm an avid planner-aheader. By the end of October, I had written in our letter that we *had already done* things scheduled for December. I reasoned that by the time my letters arrived, we would've vacationed in Las Vegas. So I included that "fact" in my missive. Wrong! Not only did we cancel our trip; the injury cancelled my whole life since I could not move from my perch on the couch.

Since then, I don't pretend to know the future. Now I say, "I'm planning on . . ." instead of arrogantly assuming I'll be alive tomorrow. This crisis taught me not to take my spouse or my future for granted. I've abandoned the notion that I can do life on my own. My prayer is that you'll learn this lesson without experiencing the pain I endured.

APPLICATION

1. Describe a time when you felt prideful, like you didn't need anyone.
2. Do you need God to "smack you down" like He did with me to make you stop taking others for granted?
3. List three people you've been taking for granted. Apologize to them. Tell them what you appreciate about them and seek ways to serve them. One day, they might be gone.

FURTHER READING: *Choosing Gratitude: Your Journey to Joy* (2011) Nancy DeMoss Wolgemuth
SONG: "God Gave Me You" (2011) by Blake Shelton

DON'T

(after having nightmares my husband divorced me.)

Please, don't depart
and break the deepest bond
one can have with another.
Don't turn away
pretending you're better off
without your other half.
Don't throw away
the years we've devoted
to the two of us together.
Please, don't forget
the cherished souvenirs,
treasures shared by me and you.
Please, stay with me
since my life would crash and burn;
since you are me and I am you.

WEEK 18

FORGIVENESS *The Prisoner It Sets Free*

To forgive is to set a prisoner free and discover that the prisoner was you.

— Lewis B. Smedes

READ: Matt. 18:21–35, Eph. 4:29–32, Col. 3:12–14

"I shouldn't have to forgive him," my friend insisted after church. "He never apologized for abusing me. He doesn't deserve it." Having never been in her shoes, I didn't know what to say. Her response is understandable. As Christians, what should our stance on forgiveness be?

According to Pastor Colin Smith, forgiveness is "a distinguishing mark of all who are in Christ, which is why the Lord teaches us to pray, 'Forgive us our sins as we forgive those who sin against us.'"

The Struggle Is Real

Most of us struggle to forgive. Especially if the offender never shows remorse. We understand the parable of the unforgiving servant. We intellectually *know* how twisted it is for people saved by grace to judge others, refusing to forgive. And yet our feelings of hurt, betrayal, and bitterness cloud our vision. Jesus told this story, found in Matthew 18 after Peter asked how many times he had to forgive those who sinned against him. Peter thought seven times would be quite generous. Jesus blew his socks off with his answer: 490 times!

What Forgiveness Isn't

Forgiveness doesn't mean trusting someone who hasn't earned that right. It's not forgoing justice, forgetting the offense, or reconciling. In fact, forgiveness isn't contingent on the perpetrator at all. It's the powerful act of releasing the burden of bitterness from your mind. Hate hurts no one but yourself. The person you hate doesn't even know you're wasting time and energy on him or her. The Bible warns that allowing roots of bitterness to grow opens the door for the Enemy. Austin Ludwig, who endured decades of abuse, said, "It takes two parties to reconcile but just one party to forgive."

What Forgiveness Is

According to Henri Nouwen, "Forgiveness is the name of love." Dr. Everett Worthington, professor emeritus of psychology, began studying the topic after his mother was murdered. He divides forgiveness into two categories. *Decisional forgiveness* involves a choice to let go of resentment toward the offender. *Emotional forgiveness* involves a shift of feelings, replacing anger with empathy.

The Benefits of Pardon

Like resting, celebrating, and being grateful, God's command to forgive is beneficial to humans. Here are some of the benefits:

- Losing our victim mentality
- Restoring agency (since we choose to forgive)
- Breaking cycles of negative rumination
- Reducing anxiety, depression, and substance abuse
- Feeling unburdened and able to start fresh

Practical Steps

Dr. Worthington developed a process involving the acronym REACH to help people forgive:

Recall (Remember the hurt objectively.)

Empathize (Try to understand the offender's viewpoint and circumstances.)

Altruism (Bring to mind times when you were forgiven.)

Commit (Publicly forgive the person who wronged you.)

Hold on (Remind yourself that you chose to forgive.)

Corrie ten Boom spent years in a Nazi concentration camp. In a November 1972 edition of Guideposts, she told the following story. A former guard (who didn't recognize her) approached her after she spoke on forgiveness in 1946. He thanked her for the message and extended his hand. But she couldn't move. She begged God to enable her to forgive him. "As I took his hand . . . a current seemed to pass from me to him, while into my heart sprang a love for this stranger that almost overwhelmed me. . . . I discovered that it is not on our forgiveness any more than on our goodness that the world's healing hinges, but on His. When He tells us to love our enemies, He gives, along with the command, the love itself."[2]

APPLICATION

1. What are the hardest things you've had to forgive?
2. What benefits has forgiveness brought you?
3. Who do you still need to forgive? Work through the REACH process for each individual.

FURTHER READING: *The Gift of Forgiveness* (1987)
Charles Stanley

SONG: "Forgiveness" (2012) by Matthew West

LET US BE A CHANNEL OF YOUR MERCY
(to the tune of "Day by Day and with Each Passing Moment")

Let us be a channel of your mercy.
Let us be your instruments of peace.
Where there's hatred, let us show compassion.
Where there's worry, set our minds at ease.
Where there's hurt, may we give true forgiveness.
Where there's doubt, may we sow seeds of faith.
In despair, may hope become a lighthouse;
in this tempest, let us light the way.
When our souls are burdened down with sorrow,
when our minds are doubting You are there,
may we spread the oil of joy and gladness,
sending angels with our whispered prayers.
May we strive to understand our neighbor.
May we seek first off to understand.
May we focus all our thoughts on loving,
giving thanks for blessings from your hand.
Oh, dear Lord, our one and only Master,
walk with us in this forsaken land.
In humility, we find true purpose,
and in dying find the Promised Land.
May your comfort be our consolation,
weaving tears and trials in our lives.
Make us holy; fit our hearts for heaven,
till our souls to golden shores arrive.

POSSESSIONS *The Joy of Letting Go*

Every heart needs to be set free

From possessions that hold it so tight.

'Cause freedom's not found in the things that we own.

It's the power to do what is right . . .

And we can't imagine the freedom we find

From the things we leave behind.

— Michael Card

READ: Matt. 19:16–30, Luke 12:13–34, 1 Tim. 6:6–10; 17–19

On a recent mission trip, I donated a bag of clothes to the church's "store" for refugees. Giving away half of my suitcase's contents literally lightened my load! Moving through airports with less stuff weighing me down was a breeze.

Dad was a bit of a hoarder. He scrubbed every baby food jar and repurposed it to hold hardware. He saved every rubber band "just in case." A scarcity mindset scarred many of his generation. Although their economic woes ended after World War II, many still hoard out of fear. But in most cases, "just in case" means "never."

Recently, I read Julia Ubbenga's book *Declutter Your Heart and Your Home*. Stuffed with clutter, Julia's home reflected her heart—filled with anxiety and disorder. Stressed, she reached for her Bible. Two concepts from Luke 12 jumped off the page: "Life does not consist in an abundance of possessions," and "Be rich in what matters" (most versions say to be rich toward God).[3] These verses changed her life. She concluded that living with less would give her more energy to focus on what mattered most.

A recent study showed we only regularly use 20 percent of the items we own. Think of that bin of cords. You don't even know what they go to. How about that CD collection? How can we divest ourselves of the 80 percent we don't use? How can we remove barriers to decluttering? Ubbenga lists three mental barriers and three emotional ones.

3 Mental Barriers

The Exposure Effect: We feel like items we see every day belong here.
The Status Quo Bias: Change is mentally perceived as loss, so we avoid it.
The Endowment Effect: We place the highest value on things we already own.

3 Emotional Barriers

Guilt: We feel bad letting go of items we spent good money on.
Fear: We're afraid we might need something later or we'll lose the memories associated with the items.
Self-Doubt: We don't believe we're capable of decluttering, so we self-sabotage with doubts.

Tools to Overcome Barriers

Remember your values: If your *family* is important, give them an uncluttered home.

Remember, memories stay when possessions go: Take photos of mementos or keep a small portion of larger sets (like one teacup).
Stop caring about other people's opinions: Once given, a gift has fulfilled its purpose of expressing love. Once given, it's none of the gift-giver's business what you do with it.
Use the 20 rule: Let it go if you can replace it for less than twenty dollars.
Use the 90/90 rule: Ask, *Have I used this in the last 90 days?* and *Will I use it in the next 90 days?*
Love your clothing: Let go of clothing that doesn't fit, needs mending, or doesn't make you feel confident when worn.

In his book *Love People, Use Things,* Joshua Fields Millburn says the easiest way to declutter is to avoid bringing stuff home. Why do we buy so many unnecessary things? Perhaps we subconsciously believe they'll make us happy. Before rushing out for retail therapy, ask yourself,

Will this add value to my life?
Would God want me to spend His money on this?
Will this make my home more peaceful?
Would I be willing/able to pay cash for this?

Our lives shouldn't center around collecting possessions for others to inherit. Shopping can never fill the God-shaped hole in our hearts. Remember, if you can't give it away, you don't own *it. It* owns you.

APPLICATION

1. What's most important to you? Do your spending and storing habits match your stated priorities?
2. Write out your own three-sentence eulogy. What do you want to be remembered for?
3. Which of the six barriers resonates with you most? Which tools will you use this week?

FURTHER READING: *Declutter Your Heart and Your Home: How a Minimalist Life Yields* **Maximum Joy (2025) by Julia Ubbenga**

SONG: "Things We Leave Behind" (1994) by Michael Card

SIMPLICITY

We work our fingers to the bone,
somehow feeling we control
the sovereign hand of Providence.
We hoard our wealth to sidestep shortage,
denying burial vaults lack storage.
And so we play the world's game.
We leave no margins on our page
and use production just to gauge
intrinsic, inherent value.
May we unearth real liberty,
birthed from calm simplicity.
For *less* is *truly* much, much more.

SELF-CARE *I Only Run When Chased*

We cannot give our hearts to God and keep our bodies to ourselves.

— Elisabeth Elliot

READ: 1 Kings 19, 1 Cor. 6:19–20; 10:31

Since knee surgery, I only run when chased. Everyone knows they should eat healthy, exercise, and pray more. But who among us does a great job with self-care? I'm a disciplined person . . . when it comes to academics and punctuality. But put anything chocolate in my path and I *will* eat it. In fact, I bought my sister a sign that reads, "I could give up chocolate, but I'm not a quitter."

The Minimum

Our bodies are the temple of the Holy Spirit. But what does that *mean*? For starters, it means our bodies must function well enough to serve God however He chooses. As I boarded a plane on the tarmac in Brazil, I thanked God I could navigate stairs with my luggage. For most of 2017, I couldn't. Faithfully doing physical therapy helped me get back into shape for ministry. Christians must also avoid being trapped by addictions such as smoking, vaping, alcoholism, or eating disorders. This is the bare minimum for servants of Christ.

Some say that "self-care" is unbiblical. However, Ephesians 5 encourages husbands to care for their wives as they care for their own bodies. That's a big assumption—that Christians take good care of their bodies. What might that look like for us?

Eat to Live, Not Live to Eat
God has provided us with quality fuel for our bodies. Without being legalistic, we ought to pay attention to what we eat and avoid frequently eating food that diminishes our health.

Crisis Mode
Our emotions play a big part in self-care. God has provided all we need to maintain our physical and mental health. When I found myself deep in postpartum depression, my mentor said it was okay to take antidepressants. Some might think that godly people don't get depressed. But take a look at Elijah in 1 Kings 19. He was suicidal. God prescribed rest and food. No one can thrive in crisis mode. They may survive, but it's not pretty.

Talk It Out
Processing feelings looks different for each individual. My dad was in great physical shape, but he worked too much and stuffed his feelings for most of his life. After four heart attacks, he learned that it's healthy to express emotions.

A Nap Has Been Taken in Your Honor
Dad did have one thing right. Rest. He was meticulous about "sleep hygiene" before it was a thing. Every night he went to bed at 9:30 p.m. He awoke seven hours later and took a one-hour nap at work. A sign on his office door proclaimed, "I am resting, sweetly resting. Please call again later."

Checking In

"If it ain't broke, don't fix it" may apply to certain situations, but not to physical health. We have a huge privilege. We *get* to see a doctor when we're sick and for regular checkups. Imagine never running diagnostics on your vehicle or changing the air filter. It's unwise and untenable.

APPLICATION

1. What area of self-care is God calling you to work on? What steps will you take?

2. How much quality sleep do you get? If it's fewer than eight hours, assess your sleep and adjust accordingly.

3. Have you been putting off a medical or dental appointment? List some things you want to be able to do in the future (like jogging), and care for your body so you can do them.

FURTHER READING: *Life of the Beloved: Spiritual Living in a Secular World* (1992) by Henri Nouwen

SONG: "Psalm 23 (I Am Not Alone)" (2018) by People & Songs

WILDERNESS THEOPHANY

The apex of my calling reached,
eased should have been my frantic fears.
Prayers concentrated lightning's heat,
to melt the rocks and silence jeers.
I faltered, flew to reason's edge;
I dove to dregs of deep despair,
upon depression's lonely ledge,
my mind caught in chimeric snares.
So many signs through me were done,
so zealous for my mighty God.
Then desperate threats had me undone,
melting down my frail façade.
In angst, I shouted to my Lord,
"I've not a single ounce to give!
No energy, I fight no more;
I've lost all my resolve to live."
I feel no force to soldier on;
this body's begging for a break.
No joy in the awaited dawn;
my soul, in silence, softly aches.
I hibernate perchance to dream,
pretending shreds of hope will stay.
Long hours, in the desert, stream.
Compassion's what I need today.
This gleaming Man for me has made
the fresh-baked bread my hunger craves.
Relieved, I cast right down the sum
of all my self-sufficient ways.
From strength to strength, I sojourn on.
Inspired purpose floods my heart.
I seek the wilderness, Paran;
a second wind my God imparts.

TIME *Stewarding Time Wisely*

If have too much to do, there are some items on the agenda that God did not put there. Let us submit the list to him and ask him to indicate which items we must delete. There is always time to do the will of God. If we are too busy to do that, we are too busy.

— Elisabeth Elliot

READ: Ps. 90:10–12, Eph. 5:10–20, James 4:13–16

There's nothing like believing you have a brain tumor to make you reevaluate your use of time. In 2017, I came down with a "mystery illness." Symptoms included migraines, blurred vision, and extreme fatigue. I went to every specialist imaginable. No one could cure me. I finally got an MRI to see if I had a brain tumor. While awaiting the results, I just *knew* I had a malignant tumor. (I assumed this because the same symptoms had led to my niece's diagnosis of brain cancer.)

In the Waiting

I reevaluated my priorities. I worried how my nine- and fourteen-year-old children would fare without a mom to cook for them. So I created the *Mom's Cooking Club* cookbook. I included all of our cherished family recipes and taught my kids how to make them.

As it turns out, I didn't have a brain tumor. The mystery illness went away on its own and continues to baffle medical science. But what would happen if we lived each day with such a heightened sense of urgency? Tomorrow isn't guaranteed. Responsibly using time involves slowing down to be present, pruning tasks that aren't of God, and living with an eternal perspective.

Being Truly Present

The song "Slow Me Down" talks about intentionally sifting out what vies for our time: "Will You show me now what to lose and what to keep?"[4] Speaking at the 2023 Christian Alliance for Orphans conference, CAFO President Jedd Medefind noted that our lives are full of more than we can do well. "It's a gift to be truly present with another person, and we cannot do this if we're always in a hurry," he said. As martyred missionary Jim Elliot said, "Wherever you are, be all there."

Pruning Wisely

Horticulture demonstrates the benefits of pruning out the extraneous. The Bible uses the image of God pruning off unnecessary branches to increase fruitfulness. Without pruning, grapevines produce small, bitter grapes. But pruning ensures better fruit. If we try to do too much, we risk becoming "jacks of all trades and masters of none."

I once visited the grave of my great-great-grandfather Heinrich Grovert. He immigrated to Iowa from Germany in 1854 at age twenty-two. My heart swelled as I read his spiritual legacy engraved in German on his tombstone: "Here rests in God . . . II Tim. 4:7–8" which reads, "I have fought the good fight, I have finished the race, and I have remained faithful."

We must fix our eyes on Jesus as we run this marathon called life. Imagine eternity as an infinite line stretching around the globe. Now put a dot on that line. The dot represents our entire life. We must invest our time in things that will matter forever. As C. T. Studd put it, "Only one life, 'twill soon be past. Only what's done for Christ will last. And when I am dying, how happy I'll be if the lamp of my life has been burned out for Thee."

APPLICATION

1. If you only had five years to live, what would you prioritize?
2. How are you stewarding the time God has lent you? What habits or hobbies waste a lot of time? Plan your schedule prayerfully this month.
3. Reflect on godly goals for your life. How can you move closer to accomplishing what matters most to God?

FURTHER READING: *Unhurried: An Invitation to Slow Down, Create Margin, and Surrender* **Control to God (2025) by Samantha Decker**

SONG: "Slow Me Down" (2023) by The Porter's Gate

THE RACE

I seek You in my sadness.
Lord, I long to glimpse Your face.
I'm running from myself, my Friend,
and from Your warm embrace.

I'm rushing back to rote routine
without a thought of You,
my focus fixed on my own needs,
O, mold my mind anew.

My soul can't serve because
distractions offer alibis.
O, break my heart with what breaks Yours;
erase these evil lies.

Loosing weights of time and pain,
pure joy now fills my heart.
Focused on my future now;
with loved ones I'll not part.

With only half a race to run,
my eyes no longer roam.
The sin I've sown is slung aside—my heart has hobbled home.

HOPE *Our Anchor in Life's Storms*

Hope itself is like a star—not to be seen in the sunshine of prosperity, and only to be discovered in the night of adversity.

— Charles Spurgeon

READ: Lam. 3:22–33, 1 Cor. 15:12–28, Heb. 6:18–20

March 2020 pulled the world into death's aura, forcing people to contemplate their mortality. When people began dying from COVID, many of my non-Christian friends were panicking! They were hoping that our government, researchers, and scientists would keep them safe from this deadly disease.

Death Is a Doorway

But as Christians, we're not blown about by scary headlines or worried about dying. Ultimately, we know that, because we're forgiven, the best is yet to come. First Corinthians 15:19 says that "if our hope in Christ is only for this life, we are more to be pitied than anyone in the world." But the converse is also true. If our hope in Christ guarantees eternal salvation, we're in the enviable position of having assurance of peace with God.

For believers, dying is like a child falling asleep in a car, having his dad carry him to bed, and waking up in his bedroom. Death is merely a doorway. As Keith Getty wrote in the song "In Christ Alone," believers have "no guilt in life, no fear in death."[5]

Hope Is an Anchor

I recently attended a parenting workshop. While the speaker's talk was beneficial, one thing she said gave me pause. She said that faith means saying, "I believe this *can* happen," and "hope" means saying, "I believe this can happen *for me*." Wait. Doesn't Hebrews 6:19 give us a better picture of hope? It says hope is "an anchor for our souls." This means that because Jesus intercedes for us with the Father, we can rest assured that God will forgive us and bring us home to heaven.

Beneath the crescent moon and palmetto tree on South Carolina license plates, there's an inspirational phrase: "While I breathe, I hope." The state motto since 1776, it serves as a testimony to hope amidst adversity. With over two hundred Revolutionary War battles fought on their soil, early Americans needed a reminder that while God was still lending them breath, they could have hope. There's nothing dead in our lives that God cannot raise.

Returning from the workshop, I wrote "Hope is an ANCHOR" on my journal page and drafted the song below. Without confidence that God will fulfill His promises, everyone would be like unmoored boats, lost at sea with no lighthouse to beckon them home.

APPLICATION

1. How confident are you that when you die, you'll go to heaven? Why?

2. Are you scared about the future of our planet? Are you worried your story won't end well? If so, find and memorize a Bible verse to calm you.

3. List ways God has protected you, provided for you, and proven his faithfulness to you in the past. God never changes. He'll prove faithful to all who hope in him.

FURTHER READING: *Hope When Your Heart Is Breaking: Finding God's Presence in Your Pain* (2021) by Ron Hutchcraft

SONG: "Hope in Front of Me" (2014) by Danny Goeke

HOPE IS AN ANCHOR (an original hymn)

Hope is an anchor; death is a doorway.
Life is a journey; faith will take flight.
Longing and yearning, looking to Jesus,
living the long view, His Kingdom in sight.

CHORUS
Praise the Lord! Heavens rejoice!
Crown Him Lord! Heed the sound of His voice!
Pain will be ended when death is no more
on that beautiful, heavenly shore.

Standing together, watching and waiting,
clinging to peace in storms of regret,
Yahweh is with us, comforting, guiding,
healing the heartaches we hope to forget.

Raising the anthem, paradise beckons,
under His banner, we're lost in His love.
Jesus is making magnificent mansions,
calling us homeward to glory above.

Walk now together, light up the darkness,
clothed with compassion, gilded with grace,
eyes to the heavens, tears turn to triumph,
fears are forgotten beholding His face.

PARENTING *Gems Mined from Heartache*

Tragic mistakes are often made by those who acquire the reins of control before their maturity is adequate to handle it.

— James Dobson

READ: 1 Kings 17:8–24, Ps. 127:3–5, Eph. 6:1–4

I've been a parent for twenty-three years. I can't imagine not having kids. In his wisdom, God only gave us two children. They're smart, stubborn, and strange. Two is all we can handle. While this lesson applies most to parents of teens, anyone can learn from my experiences.

Protect Them

God gives kids parents to protect and nurture them, preparing them for successful adulthood. Kids should thank parents for the sweat, blood, and tears we invest in them (not to mention time and money). However, children often act like brats. They get angry at us for establishing loving boundaries that prevent them from hurting themselves.

In 1 Kings 17, the widow of Zarephath blamed Elijah for her son's death. Similarly, parents are often accused by the (immature) people we serve. We can't take their negative attitudes to heart.

We're responsible before God to bring them to church, protect their innocence, and show them how to persevere when life gets hard.

Pay Attention

Henri Nouwen said, "Our children are our most important guests, who enter into our home, ask for careful attention, stay for a while and then leave to follow their own way. Children are strangers whom we have to get to know. They have their own style, their own rhythm and their own capacities for good and evil."

In an age of screens and working from home, we need to pay special attention to our kids. To nurture them, we must be present with them, paying attention to their (sometimes crazy) preferences. A hallmark of great parenting is the ability to recite all the ponies from *My Little Pony* or the trains from *Thomas & Friends*. Though annoying, it shows children we care about them as individuals.

We need to demonstrate their importance by putting down our phones and interacting with them. When they want to show us something, they're inviting us into their world, taking a step closer. We shouldn't put them off. We only have them for a limited time.

Wanting to Be Wanted

Gary Chapman's five love languages include quality time, words of affirmation, gifts, acts of service, and physical touch. Parents need to be affectionate and affirming so kids don't seek love in the arms of others. We need to discover our kids' love languages and speak them daily. Packing my child's lunch doesn't make him feel loved if his love language is quality time.

My dad didn't grow up in an affectionate family. But daughters need their dads to hold their hand, hug them, and tell them they're beautiful. This male affirmation is essential. Lacking this, I always "needed" to have a boyfriend and struggled to feel confident without one.

Adulting 101

Kids these days seem less capable and self-reliant. Our parents worked on farms and in stores before finishing high school. Many of us worked part-time jobs or babysat. Now many kids are growing up with few practical "adult" skills. We can't afford to raise children who drown in two feet of water or give up at the drop of a hat. We need to train them to manage money, conflict, and careers. Before leaving the nest, they should know how to cook, do laundry, and pay bills. This prepares them to be responsible, helpful spouses. No one wants to marry a needy baby.

Encouragement

With God's help, we can parent well. But in this fallen world, prodigals go astray in spite of our best efforts. God was the perfect parent, but it didn't guarantee that His children, the Israelites, would "turn out well." When parenting doesn't go as planned, it doesn't mean we've failed or that God has. We don't control our kids' choices or the results they get. We must entrust our kids to our Father's providential care.

Don't lose heart. Though tedious and thankless, parenting is a crucial job. Charles Sprugeon said to parents, "You are as much serving God in looking after your own children, training them up in God's fear, and minding the house . . . as you would be if you had been called to lead an army to battle for the Lord of Hosts."

APPLICATION

1. If you are a parent, do you ever feel guilty for "messing up" your children? We all do the best we can. Good parenting doesn't guarantee kids will "turn out right." Ask God to take away this unhelpful guilt. Take a moment to pray for your kids.

2. Think of a child or young person in your life. Figure out what their love language is and make a plan to "speak" it this week.

3. Parenting is a thankless job. It can be discouraging. Sometimes, we are unjustly blamed by those we love. This week, resolve to rely on God for your self-worth and refuse to get bogged down by unwarranted criticism.

FURTHER READING: *Habits of the Household* (2021)
Justin Whitmel Earley

SONG: "Remember Me" (2000) by Mark Schultz

WHAT SHE CAN BECOME

I'm weary of my flailing child.
I feel disheartened to the core.
I know she'll shoot her foot again—
those self-inflicted chosen wounds.
I'm not sure if I want control,
I know I sure don't have it.
I love and long to keep her close,
and shelter her with wise advice.
I'm so perplexed when she insists
on authoring her own mistakes.
The year is new, and I must be
remade to show what's possible.
I must get my act composed,
give up on pulling puppet strings.
I'll cast a vision and let go,
imagining on her behalf
the butterfly she can become.

COMPARISON *You Always Lose*

Comparison is the thief of joy.

— Theodore Roosevelt

READ: Rom. 12, 2 Cor. 10:12, Gal. 6:4

Even as a seasoned Christian, I still find myself comparing myself negatively to others. At a recent conference, the speaker was in her sixties. However, I couldn't stop looking at her high-waisted capris. The woman didn't have a hint of a muffin top after several children! *How is this possible?* I thought. Don't ask me what she said during her talk. I got distracted.

Our pastor, Colin Smith, told us never to compare ourselves with others. He explained that we would either end up feeling superior to others or inferior. Both are harmful. Feeling superior causes us to act condescendingly and become prideful. When we open the door to envy, it tanks our self-esteem and steals contentedness.

In his book *The Search for Significance*, Robert S. McGee identifies four core lies many people believe about themselves:[6]

- *I must meet certain standards in order to feel good about myself.* (like getting good grades)
- *I must be approved (accepted) by certain others to feel good about myself.* (like your parents or peer group)

- *Those who fail are unworthy of love and deserve to be punished.* (This shows up in people with perfectionistic parents.)
- *I am what I am, I cannot change, and I am hopeless.* (like believing that even God can't transform your life)

Superiority Complex

When we compare ourselves with others and feel superior, it feeds the instinctual sin of pride. Maybe we think we're more attractive, smarter, or better at raising kids. We raise our eyebrows and judge others. Remember, God opposes the proud. Do we want the Almighty working against us? In humility, we must realize that every person we encounter can teach us something.

Inferiority Complex

My mom, who was in her seventies, took my young daughter swimming. My six-year-old daughter studied her grandmother's legs. "Grandma, why did you write in blue pen all over your legs?" This innocent question about varicose veins did nothing to increase Mom's confidence.

Similarly, I got depressed when a well-meaning soul at church asked me when my baby was due . . . when my baby was two weeks old! Feeling fat, underprivileged, or stupid comes naturally to us. How can we combat comparison's unwanted effects?

It could be you. Remember the cliché, "There, but for the grace of God, go I." If we encounter someone who lacks intelligence, we should keep in mind that we're all one concussion away from being unable to function cognitively.

Run your own race. The Bible tells us to run the race set before us in a way that wins the prize. We cannot perform well if we drift into another runner's lane or focus on *her* race instead of our own.

You're God's masterpiece. A glance at Psalm 139 or Ephesians 2:10 tells us so. God has planned good works for each individual to do based on their unique gifting.

Avoid the people-pleasing trap. We need to care less about what others think of us and more about *God's* evaluation.

Take a break. Envy creeps in through social media, magazines, and shows depicting impossible standards. Social media snippets show the very best of people's lives. When we compare that to our normal lives, depression about our lack of money, vacations, etc. can creep in. Consider taking time off from social media.

Cultivate contentment. When I feel unattractive, I thank God for the healthy body I have. It allows me to go on mission trips, have children, and help others. Focus on the blessings God has given *you*.

Author Cindy Lee says that if an adult knows *their* worth, they'll recognize value in *others*. Godly, confident individuals have their "love tank" filled by God. They're not emotionally needy since their self-esteem doesn't rely on being needed. This frees them to turn their gaze from themselves to a world in need of Jesus.

APPLICATION

1. When comparing yourself to others, do you most often feel superior or inferior? Choose two tips from above and put them into practice this week.
2. Pick one of the four core lies from McGee's book and memorize a Bible verse to combat it.
3. Take a break from anything that induces you to make comparisons.

FURTHER READING: *The Search for Significance: Seeing Your True Worth Through God's Eyes* (2003) by Robert S. McGee

SONG: "Priceless" (2014) by for King & Country

BACKYARD LIFE

My yard is stunning and revolting,
calming and distressing,
inspiring and depressing.
I can focus on the drone of alien cicadas,
noise from lawnmowers and leaf blowers,
cars whizzing by.
I can focus on sparrows' harsh chirping,
flies landing on food, bare patches of dirt,
on tidbits of trash, the dusty birdfeeder,
weeds choking my perennials.

Or I can see my yard as a sanctuary . . .

where silver maples shade my chair,
bluegrass breathes life into my lungs,
where goldfinches bathe in secret pools,
nuthatches cling to bumpy bark,
cardinals "birdy, birdy" at the top of tulip trees,
and daylilies reach for their song,
where crimson king maples reign, dark against the azure sky.

This is my life. On what shall I focus?

WHO KILLED JESUS? *Contributing to Christ's Suffering*

It was my sin that held Him there until it was accomplished.

— Stuart Townsend

READ: Matt. 27:14, 11–26, John 10:14–19, Acts 2:22–36

When I lived in France, I heard a fascinating sermon entitled "Who Killed Jesus?" You may smirk at how philosophical the French are, but the question remains.

The Jews
If we were playing Family Feud, the most popular response to this question would likely be "the Jews." The corrupt leaders who believed Yeshua was a blasphemer. The high priest's temple guards arrested Jesus before His crucifixion. Therefore, "the Jews" bear responsibility for killing Christ.

Pontius Pilate
"But wait," you might say, "Pontius Pilate should've listened to his wife when she warned him about Christ's innocence. He could've prevented Christ's death." But Pilate cared more about keeping the peace than about justice. In a weak attempt to soothe his guilty

conscience, he "washed his hands" of the whole debacle (Matt. 27:24). By then it was too late.

Roman Soldiers

Who did the dirty work? Who pounded seven-inch spikes through his wrists? The same scoundrels who punctured his scalp with a crown of thorns and ran him through with a sword. A strong case can be made that Roman soldiers killed Christ.

Judas Iscariot

For many, the first person who springs to mind as responsible is Judas Iscariot. Greedy for silver and disheartened by the Messiah's lack of political ambition, Judas played his part in Christ's betrayal.

God

Now we must wade into the depths of divine sovereignty. Who ultimately pulls all the strings in the universe? God. Who sent us an atoning sacrifice for our sins? God the Father loved the world so much that He sent his precious Son to save us (John 3:16).

Jesus

But wait, in the Garden of Gethsemane, sweating blood, Jesus could've called the whole thing off. While on the cross, He could've commanded angels to rescue Him. Instead, He proclaimed that *He himself* gave up His life willingly. Jesus understood His terrifying mission when he took on flesh. *He chose* to become our Passover Lamb.

Adam/Eve and Satan

And *why* did Jesus have to die? Because of the fall. Sin entered the world when Satan deceived Adam and Eve and they rebelled against God. This makes the first couple, and the Father of Lies who tempted them, responsible for Jesus' death.

You, Me, and Everyone

So far, several entities are to blame for Christ's death. But the final and most poignant answer to our question expands the scope. Who killed Jesus? You did. I did. We all did.

We all killed Christ. So, never let a hint of anti-Semitism creep into your theology. Groups throughout history have discriminated against Jews because "they" killed Christ. But without Judaism, there *is no* Christianity. Jews penned every single book of the Bible (minus Luke and Acts). In the first century, the burning question was, "Can you be a good Christian *without* following Jewish law?"

As a young adult, I watched *The Passion of the Christ*. I witnessed a realistic portrayal, in technicolor, of Christ gushing blood, battered beyond recognition, dying for my sins. A weight sank to the bottom of my stomach. It was *my* sin that held him there. Every sin we've ever committed and every sin we *will* commit killed the Lord of Lords. After seeing how the evil in my heart made Christ suffer, I even foolishly tried not to sin for a few days. If you've ever tried to go twenty-four hours without sinning, you know it's impossible.

APPLICATION

1. Before reading this, who did you believe was most responsible for killing Christ? What do you think now and why?
2. When you think about your sin holding Christ to the cross, how do you feel? Take a moment to confess any sinful actions or attitudes.
3. Have you ever held any anti-Semitic opinions? If so, ask the Messiah to forgive you. Research a Jewish holiday mentioned in Scripture and learn how it relates to Christians.

FURTHER READING: *The Case for Christ: A Journalist's Personal Investigation of the Evidence* **for Jesus (1998) Lee Strobel**

SONG: "We Are the Reason" (1980) by David Meece

BEFORE I GAZED UPON THE LORD

(an original song to the tune of
"When I Survey the Wondrous Cross")

Before I gazed upon the Lord,
arrogance swelled within my chest.
But when I felt His crimson blood,
I fell down, prostrate, in the dust.
Seeing salvation lifted up,
for suffering souls who turn to Him,
I know I could not take this cup
or hope my home in heaven to win.
Through my hurt, Christ's compassion bleeds,
mingling with solemn sacrifice.
To form crowns fit for such as He,
Earth's bright rainbows can't suffice.
My soul, my life, my all are His;
all pales compared to Calvary's gift.
And every treasure that exists
could not repay a love like this.

HOSPITALITY *Invited to Belong*

Hospitality means primarily the creation of free space where the stranger can enter and become a friend instead of an enemy. Hospitality is not to change people but to offer them space where change can take place. It is not to bring men and women over to our side, but to offer freedom not disturbed by dividing lines.

— Henri Nouwen

READ: Rom. 12:9-16; 16:1–7, 1 Tim. 5:9–10, Heb. 13:1–3

Rations

In 1993, I went with some French Christians to Romania for the wedding of two of Dad's former students. The bride was French, and the groom was from Arad. The Berlin Wall had only fallen four years prior. Formerly Communist countries were still recovering from subjugation. We drove past wheat fields being harvested by a horse and cart. Though they had little, Romanian believers volunteered to host three guests each. Each quaint home had a wrought iron gate, a pergola laden with grapevines, and a linden tree.

Though I was only nineteen, these Evangelicals honored me as an important guest. They gave me sugar for my linden tea and sausage they had saved when rationed. They weren't wealthy, but their rich hospitality warmed my lonely heart. It made me realize that, as part of God's family, I have everything I need.

I could tell stories of Christians hosting me in the DRC, in Jamaica, in France, and in India. The beauty of our membership in Christ's family is that we can go anywhere in the world and be welcomed by strangers who love the Lord.

Belonging

In his book *The Life We're Looking For,* Andy Crouch describes the hospitality shown by Gaius, referenced in Romans 16:23. The whole church had enjoyed Gaius's hospitality. What did this Roman head of household living in Corinth do that was so revolutionary? Gaius welcomed slaves, women, noncitizens, and Jews into his home and into his spiritual family. These unrelated guests called one another "brother" and "sister." Crouch describes the "ideal human community" in which every single member matters as much as each part of our own bodies matters to us. He asserts that the New Testament upheaval of social stratification turned the world upside down.[7]

Diversity and Unity

In 2014, the executive pastor of our EFCA church, Scott Lothery, preached on Romans 16. He noted that those Paul greeted included males, females, couples (Andronicus and Junia), singles (Mary), slaves (Persus), Jews (Aquila), and Africans (Rufus). Showing hospitality begins with valuing individuals, not discriminating against them.

Edith Schaeffer sums it up well in *The Hidden Art of Homemaking.* "The tight little segregated life, always spent with people your own age, economic group, educational background, and culture tends to bring an ingrown, static sort of condition. Fresh ideas, reality of communication and shared experiences will be sparks to light up fires of creativity, especially if the people spending time together are a true cross-section of ages, nationalities, kindred, and tongues."[8]

Valued

I love greeting people at church. As a language nerd, I attempt to greet everyone in their native tongue. Over the years, I've greeted people in twenty-five languages. What does smiling and greeting someone in their heart language do? It demonstrates respect for their culture. It makes them feel cherished. The goal of Christian hospitality is to treat others as Christ would, to serve them gladly, and to share with those in need.

Gaius likely hosted many missionaries and travelers over the years. I doubt he complained about how much it cost or how inconvenient it was. As Gaius blessed others with his open heart and home, he likely received more than he gave.

APPLICATION

1. Are you an extrovert or an introvert? Introverts can be hospitable too. Brainstorm three ways you can welcome others this week. Consider a board game night for introverts.
2. Even if you live in a tiny apartment, you can show Christ's love by inviting others over to be heard and cared for. A warm beverage and a compassionate heart are all it takes. If you've been perfectionistic, not wanting to host unless your home is perfect, give it up today.
3. How can you grow this week in treating other believers as family?

FURTHER READING: *The Hidden Art of Homemaking* **(1985) Edith Schaeffer**

SONG: "Home" (1994) by Michael Card

THE BEST MEAL

We ladies have a schedule for meals for new mothers.
Excited at girls' night out, expecting what I *knew* was a girl,
I wore a smile and light pink.
The next day, as pink bled to red, my heart again broke.
My husband, my father, my son could not grasp
the depth of my loss.
Then at my door arrived a meal and a sympathy card.
Mostaccioli. I don't even like mostaccioli,
but it was the best meal I've ever tasted,
compassion being the richest fare.

LESSONS FROM COVID *Essential*

For "the household of God," this judgment from God is purifying, not punitive—not punishment.... It is discipline, not destruction.

— John Piper

READ: Prov. 16:9, Col. 2:13–23, Heb. 12:1–3

In 2022, I made a list of both the benefits of COVID and what the pandemic taught me. Benefits included getting takeout from sit-down restaurants and not having to interact with pizza delivery guys. Here are some of the lessons I learned in the school of COVID.

Who/What Is Essential?

Some jobs are 100 percent unnecessary. Remember the term "essential personnel"? It applied primarily to medical professionals and public safety officials. In the thick of COVID, networks canceled live sports competitions. Pre-pandemic, I was a football widow half of the time. I was thrilled when sports stopped clogging up our schedule. Hollywood stopped creating new movies and TV shows. Now the cat is out of the bag! In the hierarchy of important professions, entertainers rank low on the totem pole. Actors and sports celebrities are superfluous diversions. The absence of new shows proved beneficial. A trend arose in the ashes of mindless entertainment: family members spending time together. Reading, playing board games, talking, making meals, telling stories. As John Piper prayed, "Do not waste our misery and grief, O Lord. Purify your people from powerless preoccupation with barren materialism and Christless entertainment."

Hold Schedules Loosely

My brother mocks me for planning too far ahead. I chide him for flying by the seat of his pants. Once, I asked him what country he planned to reside in the following month. He had no idea. The year 2020 gave planners a swift kick in the head. Within days, COVID erased our schedules. No church, no eating out, no vacationing.

During lockdowns, the whole world pressed the pause button. We received a once-in-a-lifetime opportunity to clear our schedules and thoughtfully put the big rocks (priorities) back in first. Post COVID, author David Hollis advised, "In the rush to return to normal, use this time to consider which parts of 'normal' are worth rushing back to."

One Giant Leap for Technology

Necessity is the mother of invention. Millions of children needed to continue learning during the pandemic. I was teaching French during COVID. Some students attended in person while others "Zoomed" in for classes. So, I received a Zoom account and learned to use it. Because of this technology, my students had the unprecedented privilege of interviewing a Senegalese boy live in class.

Rewrite Holiday Rules

Easter 2020 came on the heels of COVID lockdowns. Barred from attending church or family gatherings, we took the opportunity to whittle the holiday down to its essence. Though I'm the youngest, I'm frequently forced to host holiday gatherings. I prepare a ham, along with an alternative dish because so-and-so can't have ham. I whip up a feast and then scramble to arrive at a packed church in time to have seats.

But COVID made me wonder why Easter should center around preparing a meal I don't want to make or eat. Coronavirus Easter was the best! No dressing up or harassing kids to get ready. No cooking. And best of all, no vacuuming up shreds of plastic Easter grass three years later. After sifting out the commercialized chaff, we retained only the most meaningful parts. Consequently, after an inspiring sermon in 2020, I ordered pizza. That's right. Easter *pizza*. *Can she do that?* you wonder. She *can* and she *did*.

That year, warm and snug in our family room, I felt at peace. I relished a simpler holiday stripped of bells and whistles. Easter morphed into something more intimate and sacred than before. I learned that holidays are whatever we want them to be. For once in our lives, COVID allowed us to simply be *us*—together yet apart from the crowd—focused on the presence of our risen Lord.

APPLICATION

1. List at least three things God taught you through the COVID pandemic.
2. How did being at home more, and possibly being alone more, affect you?
3. Is your job essential? How are you making an eternal impact?

FURTHER READING: *Coronavirus and Christ* **(2020) John Piper**

SONG: "The Voice of Truth" (2003) Casting Crowns

ONE UNSUSPECTING DAY IN MARCH

One unsuspecting day in March
our world came to a halt.
Our schedules were wiped clean.
Our best laid plans were stalled.
If you had told me last year
that skies would empty out,
that roads would all be carless,
I would've had my doubts.
A worldwide pandemic,
the earth's foundations swayed.
It isolated everyone
and set our lives ablaze.

MARRIAGE *Decades of Wedded Bliss?*

I have come to believe that the two most potent peace-killers are the need to be right and the need to assess blame.

— Donna Otto

READ: Deut. 24:5, Matt. 5:21–24, 18:15–17

Manage Expectations

Don't assume your spouse will act like your parents. When we were first married, I thought my husband would do all the chores like my dad. He thought I'd do everything like his homemaking grandma. Wrong.

Communicate Clearly

Our marriage started off on the wrong foot. Knute was deathly ill on our honeymoon but didn't tell me. He tried to white-knuckle it so we'd have fun. I assumed he didn't find me attractive when he didn't spend much time with me that week.

Most spouses are somewhat opposites. I'm an affectionate, extroverted oversharer who hates math. Knute is a half-Swedish, introverted undersharer who does tensor calculus for fun. We think differently. I discovered I need to give Knute time to process any new ideas I pitch to him. He learned that he has to let me know when he's resolved an issue in his mind or I'll keep harping on it.

Rate Your Feelings

Did you come from a quiet family or a bunch of yellers? Either way, it's essential to accurately communicate how important things are to you. My mom, Carol Nevin, suggests that people rate their feelings on a scale from one to ten. Like, "I really want someone to mow the lawn. I'm embarrassed an 8 out of 10 since the grass is so long."

Speak Their Love Languages, Not Just Yours

God has a sense of humor. Many spouses hate doing what makes their partner feel loved. For years, I was speaking *my* love languages of physical touch and words of affirmation to my spouse. His love languages are acts of service and gifts, so my efforts were wasted. I felt unloved without hugs and encouragement.

Don't Assume Negative Motivations

We married in 1996. In 2001, I discovered my husband had secretly been mad at me for five years. I had no idea why. Most of it involved him assuming negative motivations on my part, which he later learned were nonexistent.

Be Emotionally Healthy

Not needy. Make your home a peaceful place to be. Work on *your own* spiritual growth. Leave your spouse to God. Own up to *your* contribution to problems. Do your share of housework without keeping track or nagging. Have outside friends. Spouses cannot substitute for friends, mentors, or family members.

Don't Compete

Remember, you're on the same team. Ecclesiastes 4:12 says that someone standing alone can be defeated but that two people together can rout enemies. Resist the urge to try to be right all the time. Agree to disagree. As newlyweds, we used to be competitive against each other in trivia. This isn't healthy. It's best when we work together since our strengths make up for our partner's weaknesses.

Remember Who the Enemy Is

It's natural to want to assess blame. If someone left the fridge open and the food's spoiled, it doesn't matter *who* made the mistake. Blaming is counterproductive. Just clean up the mess together. Couples should stop attacking one another. Instead, we should remember that our common enemy is Satan. Figure out what Satan wants to happen in any given situation and do the opposite.

Take the Initiative

At a Navigators marriage retreat, we learned that "the ball is always in your court." Whether you've been sinned *against* or you sinned against *someone else*, the Bible tells us to go to the other person and work it out. Even those of us who hate conflict.

Commit

When Christians marry, they shouldn't expect to divorce. No one should separate what God joins together. We committed to never mentioning the "D word" (divorce). David Mathis wrote that although spouses will inevitably sin against one another, God designed marriage to hold them together in tough times. Scottish preacher Alistair Begg asked someone considering having an affair, "Is marriage *worse* than you expected?" The man said it was. Alistair replied, "Good. That's what you signed up for . . . for better or for worse."

APPLICATION

1. What percentage of arguments could you avoid if you gave up the desire to be right or assess blame?
2. How can you improve communication and manage expectations with loved ones this week?
3. In any conflict, ask yourself what the enemy wants to happen and do the opposite. Describe a recent conflict and how you could have applied this advice.

FURTHER READING: *The Five Love Languages: The Secret to Love that Lasts* **(1992) by Gary Chapman**
SONG: "Lead Me" (2010) by Sanctus Rea

FOR WORSE

He helps me shower on a borrowed seat.
He brings the kids to my sick bed to wish me well.
He completes the chores I should do but can't.
Holding me close, his care makes me cry harder.
In life's darkest days, he holds out hope.
A hole in my cheek, he calls me beautiful.
He helps me avoid surgery with genius ideas.
I never have to ask him to do what I need.
Through thick and thin, in sickness and health,
Thirty years of worse has made us better.

APPEARANCE GUIDELINES *Peacocking at Church*

The Bible does not call fashion or makeup or hair styling evil in and of itself. But the trajectory of the New Testament is toward simplicity and modesty and inward beauty of character and what you might call undistracting personhood-revealing—as opposed to body-revealing—apparel.

— John Piper

READ: 1 Cor. 10:23–33, 1 Tim. 2:8–10, 1 Pet. 3:3–5

On a long plane ride, I watched a cheesy romcom called *17 Again*. In it, an eccentric man develops a crush on a female school principal. One day, he shows up dressed to the nines. The principal accuses him of "peacocking." This term means to dress ostentatiously or flamboyantly in order to attract others. I wondered whether some aspects of peacocking show up in our churches on Sunday. After all, what motivates people when choosing what to wear to church?

To Pearl or Not to Pearl

Our service is live-streamed, so when I read Scripture aloud in church, I try to dress nicer than usual. One morning, I considered wearing the pearl necklace I'd purchased on a mission trip to the Philippines. Though I only paid twenty dollars for it, the same necklace would cost $800 here. I thought of 1 Timothy 2:8–10, which mentions not wearing pearls to church. I know this isn't meant to be taken literally in our culture. However, I believe the overarching principle is to avoid flaunting wealth or turning church into a fashion show. Worship isn't about us, so there's no need to draw undue attention to ourselves.

Modesty

This passage also says women should dress modestly. This concept is contextual. In each culture and era, modesty is redefined. Here's an example. In the U.S., most conservative Christian women wear one-piece bathing suits. In Saudi Arabia, that would be beyond immodest. When visiting France, I was stunned to discover that there, evangelicals often wear bikinis. Why? Because many non-Christian women go topless at French beaches. It's all relative.

How can Christian women and girls dress modestly? One way to think about it is, "If it ain't for sale, don't advertise it." What I mean is that, unless seeking a sexual encounter, there's no reason to intentionally dress sensually. Dress beautifully and confidently . . . but not sexy. It saddens me to see sisters in Christ wearing short skirts, leggings that show every curve, or low-cut tops. Especially at church. As a female, even *I'm* distracted when people dress immodestly. When someone wears a miniskirt or bears her shoulders or back in church, it's distracting. I can't even imagine how disruptive it must be for men.

When dressing, Christians ought to ask, *What's my motivation?* When attending church, our goal should be to look clean, respectful, and put-together. We should focus more on internal beauty than on externals. We shouldn't be flaunting diamond earrings, gold chains, or designer handbags. We wouldn't want to draw attention away from Christ or make others feel bad.

Finally, we should be willing to give up our rights in order to help others get closer to God. If wearing flashy jewelry or showing too much skin is liable to cause a fellow believer to stumble, we should forgo it even if it's not expressly prohibited in Scripture.

APPLICATION

1. When you dress for church, what motivates you to select certain clothing?
2. Do you think it's sinful to wear an expensive watch or shoes? How does the person's intent or location factor into your answer?
3. What permanent principles can you apply from what you read today? How should you handle it if someone else is dressing in a distracting manner at church? Whatever your response, if the person is female, have a *female* discuss it with her (not a male).

FURTHER READING: *Modest: Men and Women Clothed in the Gospel* (2012) by R. W. Glenn and Tim Challies

SONG: "Picture Perfect" (1992) by Michael W. Smith

WANTING TO BE WANTED

A fool can see what's up for sale;
a fool can feel the longing.
Behind the sparkly, skimpy clothes,
young women seek belonging.
They hike their hems to primp and pose,
lining pouty, glossy lips.
Hoping for a decent bloke,
they lower necklines, swivel hips.
They wonder if he notices.
Sadness lurks behind their eyes.
They sell themselves to dull the pain,
seductive smiles concealing lies.
They can't face themselves in mirrored bars
or contemplate deep questions.
The pub is closing; call a car
and pray they learn their lesson.

WORKS VS. GRACE *Witnessing to "Good" People*

No man knows how bad he is till he has tried very hard to be good.

— C. S. Lewis

READ: Rom. 3:21–28, Eph. 2:1–10, Tit. 3:3–7

We sat around the table at Awana. I asked the girls if they thought they'd go to heaven when they died. They all said they would. "Why?" I inquired. A sweet blonde answered, "Because I'm a good person." We've all heard this classic line of thought. "I've never killed anyone or committed adultery." But if people could earn their way to heaven by being good, why did Christ have to die?

Imagine heaven is Hawaii (not too difficult to do) and we all start off on the California coast. To get to heaven/Hawaii, everyone must swim. Strong swimmers will get closer to Hawaii, but no one will make it on their own. If we're talking good works, Mother Teresa would get pretty far, but even she couldn't make it.

I understand why people think they're "mostly good." Most religions teach that humans can work our way to heaven. Like some moral highway to God. Let's look at salvation from the perspective of the world's major religions.

Islam—Follow the Five Pillars of Islam:

Shahada – a declaration of faith stating that there's no God but Allah and that Mohammed is his prophet

Salah – praying five times a day facing Mecca

Sakat – giving to charity

Sawm – ritual fasting from dawn to dusk during Ramadan

Hajj – making a pilgrimage to Mecca

Catholicism—Do the following:

Receive Christ as Savior by faith

Be baptized in the Trinitarian formula

Be infused with additional grace by observing Catholic sacraments (including Confirmation, Eucharist, Reconciliation/Penance, Anointing the Sick, Marriage, and Holy Orders)

Die without any unconfessed mortal sins

Hinduism—Pick a path to liberation from reincarnation and become one with the divine:

The way of works— earning good karma through religious duty

The way of knowledge—realizing that the one True Self (Brahman) is everywhere

The way of devotion—worshipping a specific deity

All of these religions are represented by a hand reaching up to heaven, trying to earn salvation. In biblical Christianity, however, it's God's hand that reaches down to save us—because we could never earn salvation. As D. L. Moody put it, "God has nothing to say to the self-righteous. Unless you humble yourself before Him in the dust, and confess before Him your iniquities and sins, the gate of heaven, which is open only for sinners, saved by grace, must be shut against you forever."

Back to Awana. I challenged the girls, "Try to go twenty-four hours without sinning." I reminded them that sin includes *doing* bad things, *thinking* bad things, *saying* bad things, and *not* doing the good we should do. I wished them well. Surprise. Not one girl could go a single day without sinning . . . and neither could I.

APPLICATION

1. Try to go without sinning for twenty-four hours, keeping in mind the full definition of sin. How long did you last?
2. Have a nonthreatening conversation this week with someone who believes you can earn salvation. Tell them about your twenty-four-hour experiment.
3. Memorize three verses about salvation by grace through faith (such as Eph. 2:8–9).

FURTHER READING: *Heaven, How I Got Here: The Story of the Thief on the Cross* (2015) by Colin S. Smith

SONG: "His Mercy Is More" (2019) by Keith and Kristyn Getty and Matt Papa

---

TWENTY-FOUR HOURS OF EARNING GRACE

I tried to go without sinning¾
Twenty-four hours of earning grace.
I purposed not to steal or kill,
worship idols or fornicate.
I knew I couldn't complain at all,
or gossip, or swear, or tell lies.
I couldn't harbor hate in my heart,
be brash, be rude, or compromise.
Exhausted, I thought I was done.
Don't sin in thought or word or deed.
I was proud of my self-control.
Then, I read James 4:17.
Sin is knowing the good to do
and then failing to act on it.
I did not make it one full day.
I reverted to throwing fits.
I yelled at drivers, referees;
I lashed out at a slow cashier.
I insulted my own children
when they tried to interfere.
"I can't forgive what they have done.
He doesn't deserve my mercy."
I know I shouldn't waste the time,
Gifts, or gold that God has given me.
I found out I can't go one hour
with a pure, holy heart and mind.
No sin may enter heaven's gates,
so without grace, to hell resigned,
I kneel in repentance and thanks.

FAITH *Taking the First Step*

Faith is a living, daring confidence in God's grace, so sure and certain that the believer would stake his life on it a thousand times.

— Martin Luther

READ: Heb. 11, James 1:2–8, 1 Pet. 1:3–9

In 2017, my family and I traveled to Italy. I promised to take our kids to the island of Elba, where Napoleon was exiled. While waiting for the ferry, I had to go up to an office for information. Before me stood an escalator. It looked broken. It wasn't moving and there was no one on it. Being curious, I took a hesitant step toward the first ridged stair. Like magic, the escalator roared to life and lifted me to the second level. All I had to do was get on. The escalator did the rest.

It doesn't take faith to trust God when we're 100 percent positive things will work out. Genuine faith always requires action without having the full picture. Hebrews 11 defines faith as confidence, based on past experience, that God will continue to be good to us in the future. I extracted ten truths about faith from this chapter.

Faith believes God formed the universe. Based on God's Word and the evidence for intelligent design embedded in everything, we believe the Genesis account.

Faith follows God's directions. Abel followed God's directions for sacrifices. Without such trust, we can't please God. We cannot make up our own directions for pleasing God. We must follow His guidelines.

Faith obeys God—even when it doesn't make sense. Hebrews give the example of Noah building an ark in a land without rain.

Faith looks forward to a city with eternal foundations. As Christians, our entire earthly existence is one of faith. We're bound for heaven where God will reward those who love him. Since we're foreigners on Earth, nonbelievers will mock and misunderstand us. Faith places its hope in a better life after Christ's second coming.

Faith moves when God says to. Chris Tomlin's song "I Will Follow" says, "Where You go, I'll go; when You move, I'll move." Abram was living comfortably in Ur (southern Iraq). God commanded him to move his entire household to . . . God didn't tell him where. That takes faith! While waiting on God, he and his family lived in tents in unfamiliar territory. Submitting our will to God's means following him even when we can't see the path ahead.

Faith welcomes future blessings. Talk about advanced maternal age! Sarah believed (after initially thinking it was crazy) that God would bless her with a son even though she was ninety. God told her that hundreds of generations would descend from her long-awaited child. She welcomed God's plan.

Faith is willing to sacrifice. Abraham must have felt confused when God instructed him to sacrifice this miracle child on the altar. But Abraham climbed the mountain in faith. He knew God could raise the dead and would find a way to keep His promise.

Faith banks on God's promises. Joseph believed God would deliver his people from bondage in Egypt. He put his proverbial money where his mouth was. He commanded the Israelites to take his bones out of Egypt and bury them in the Promised Land. "[Joseph] was expected, as you and I are, to live out his life one day at a time in something less than complete understanding. What pleased God was Joseph's faithfulness when nothing made sense," said James Dobson.

Faith obeys God instead of man. In Acts 4:19, Peter and John ask those who arrested them, "Do you think God wants us to obey you rather than him?" Similarly, when a decree commanded the Israelites to give up their baby boys to be slaughtered, Moses' parents obeyed God instead. Faith doesn't fear those who can only kill the body.

Faith turns weakness into strength. God endowed people of faith like David and Daniel with His power to accomplish great things.

Sometimes God asks us to do things that seem crazy. Paint doorposts with lamb's blood. Wet your sandals in the Red Sea to walk across on dry land. As with the Italian escalator, taking the first step of faith is the hardest part. Let's choose faith instead of fear this week and boldly obey God instead of trusting our own wisdom.

APPLICATION

1. Write your own definition of faith in God. What does it require?
2. Who's your favorite Bible character who demonstrated faith? Why?
3. What are you having difficulty trusting God about? How has God proven His goodness to you in the past? Has He ever failed you? Ask God to take away your worries and fears and increase your faith.

FURTHER READING: *A Disruptive Faith: Expect God to Interrupt Your Life* (2011) by A. W. Tozer

SONG: "What Faith Can Do" (2009) by Kutless

FAITH

Faith informs us that we were created.
Faith hears God's voice and follows, persuaded.
Faith looks forward to an eternal home.
Faith knows that one day we'll know as we're known.
Faith moves whenever God says we should move.
Faith has compassion on all those God loves.
Faith welcomes a future full of good things.
Faith believes God, whatever life brings.
Faith will sacrifice what it holds dearest.
Faith holds God's hand when paths are not clearest.
Faith banks on God's promises, looking ahead.
Faith follows the light when some are misled.
Faith does not fear, though obscure be the night.
Faith transforms weaknesses into our might.

SUFFERING *When Life Knocks You Down*

If we learn to know God in the midst of our pain, we come to know Him as one who is not a High Priest that cannot be touched with the feeling of our infirmities. He is one who has been over every inch of the road. I love that old hymn by Richard Baxter, "Christ leads me through no darker rooms than He went through before."

— Elisabeth Elliot

READ: Job 42, Joel 2:21–25, 1 Pet. 5:1–11

Is This You?

Has life knocked you down? Are you in crisis mode just trying to survive, not even *dreaming* of thriving? I know how it feels when problems pile up and weigh you down. My family has endured financial crises, suicidal relatives, the loss of loved ones, and health issues for over a decade. I kept hoping our story would mirror that of Joseph. Seven good years, then seven bad years maximum. But our seven bad years turned into seventeen. If you or someone you care about feels hopeless, here's some advice I learned the hard way.

Don't Go It Alone

When crisis hits, contact your pastor, counselor, or other Christians for support. When I was at my lowest, I emailed ten pastors, begging them to pray for me. They did, and it made a difference. If you're experiencing severe depression, consult a Christian professional.

Renew Your Mind

Listening to uplifting Christian music also helped. I'm dating myself, but in my darkest times, a CD of songs with encouraging lyrics helped to alleviate my anxiety. When facing trials, we're tempted to believe God isn't good or that He's punishing us. But we know the truth. It just doesn't always feel like it. That's why it's imperative to renew our minds with biblical truth when tested. Books like *Lies Women Believe,* by Nancy DeMoss Wohlgemuth, assert that believing Satan's lies causes most problems. Memorizing Scripture to combat the lies we most frequently believe works wonders.

Make the Most of Trials

Colin Smith, our EFCA pastor for three decades, gave the following sermon illustration. You're lowered into a deep, pitch-black pit. Groping around, you feel jagged stones scattered on the ground. You can either wait idly to be rescued or gather the stones. Once you're pulled back into the light, you realize the stones you gathered in the dark are diamonds. Some gems can only be mined in dark places.

In his book *Reaching Out*, Henri Nouwen says, "Frequently . . . hunger helps us to appreciate food, and war gives us words for peace. Not seldom are our visions of the future born out of the sufferings of the present and our hope for others out of our own despair. . . . The paradox is indeed that new life is born out of the pains of the old."[9]

Who's in Charge?

The third thing that helped was setting aside time for prayer. Crying out to the only One who controls anything is the only remedy. So much happens over which we have *no control*. Our awareness of catastrophes around the globe outpaces our ability to help. This gap causes stress. The good news is that we can *always* do something effective in times of need. We can come before the throne of grace to find help and an anchor for our souls.

The Last Chapter

In the final chapter of Job, everything shifts. Job admits he understood nothing of God's plans. God sets the record straight, saying that Job's friends were wrong to doubt God's goodness. After all the suffering Job experienced, God blessed his life even more than before.

Suffering can either make us bitter or better. I'm sorry you're experiencing this dark night of the soul. I pray that God will lift you up in due time, restoring the years the locusts have eaten. After you're back in the light, I hope you will comfort others with the comfort you received.

APPLICATION

1. How stressed are you on a scale from one to ten? What's bothering you most?
2. How can you help yourself or others to find the support they need?
3. Make a list of Christian songs or verses that speak to your situation and meditate on the truth.

FURTHER READING: *Walking with God through Pain and Suffering* (2015) by Timothy Keller

SONG: "Blessed Be Your Name" (2002) by Matt Redman

THE DEEP

My wound is as deep as the sea. How to heal?
As destruction rolls over, my heart stands still.
Like the valley of death, my soul is so dry;
so thirsty, submerged in the salt, I can't cry.
Over the swells, charcoal storm clouds stacked,
drowning in crisis, my nerve melts like wax.
My life ebbs away, seven storms at a time.
In chaos, my courage dissolves in the brine.
And just when I fear that my ship will be wrecked,
You speak peace to the torrents, who bow in respect.
Inhaling relief, I take a deep breath,
newly moored in my hoped-for harbor of rest.

WEEK 33

WORRYING *Stuff Your Worries in a Sack*

Worrying is carrying tomorrow's load with today's strength—carrying two days at once. It is moving into tomorrow ahead of time. Worrying doesn't empty tomorrow of its sorrow; it empties today of its strength.

— Corrie ten Boom

READ: Ps. 94:17–19, Matt. 6:25–34, Phil. 4:6–7

"You can stuff your sorries in a sack, mister!" is a classic quote by George Costanza on the TV show *Seinfeld*. It means the apology isn't accepted. However, I prefer the phrase "Stuff your *worries* in a sack." I've struggled to keep worry at bay, but I want to share with you how I cope.

Troublesome Times

I traversed an ill-fated season of life in 2017. In December 2016, I tumbled down our stairs, severing my patellar tendon. Unable to walk, shower, or travel without assistance, my mental health took a nosedive.

In March, I glimpsed the proverbial light peeking out from behind the clouds. Then, a mystery illness left me sick through June. My symptoms included migraines, blurry vision, and extreme fatigue. Each day, I'd sleep for thirteen hours straight and still require a three-hour nap. I visited every specialist. No one ever deciphered the cause of my sickness. It came and went.

Saving Face

In September 2017, the dermatologist found skin cancer in the middle of my face. After surgery removed five layers of basal cell carcinoma, I was left with a quarter-sized hole in my right cheek. A plastic surgeon cut off the hole, reattaching my face with forty black stitches that stood out like barbed wire. Soon, facial bruises swelled, tanking my self-esteem. But some part of me felt vindicated. Sporting a giant square of gauze, I sensed that people might finally comprehend the weight of my pain. My angst hovered close to the surface. I feared that if anyone even nudged me, I'd break out sobbing.

Hang It Up

Once, I visited an aesthetician for a facial. She encouraged me to relax. In a condescending baby-talk voice, she said, "Before the facial, gather up *all* your worries and place them in this imaginary bag. Then, I'll hang the sack on this hook. You may pick your worries up before leaving. But you might not want to." It dawned on me that there might be a way to relieve my stress and sadness. A way to feel "light" again.

Two years passed. I found myself in the most tranquil place in the world— a Philippine island called Palawan. Floating in the infinity pool overlooking the ocean, I stared at cerulean skies and emerald palm fronds. I knew what needed to happen. Arms outstretched in surrender, I inhaled the tropical air. Then and there, I released my worries into the cool water. I felt them sinking to the depths, buoying my body to bask in the sun. I left my worries in that pool, and I *never* picked them up again.

APPLICATION

1. List everything you're currently worried about.
2. Memorize Philippians 4:6–7 in your favorite version.
3. Tell God what you need and thank Him for all He's done. Pay attention to the peace this brings to your heart.

FURTHER READING: *Anxious for Nothing: Finding Calm in a Chaotic World* (2017) **by Max Lucado**

SONG: "Firm Foundation (He Won't)" (2023) by Cody Carnes

DON'T WORRY

Don't worry about anything,
but ask the Lord for everything.
Tell your Creator all you need,
and thank Him for His selfless deeds.
And so, you'll sense the peace of God
come washing through you like a flood.
Remembering that heaven reigns,
that Providence controls all things,
will guard your heart and calm your mind,
and certain solace, you will find.
Do not be anxious, trust the Lord.
Cast your cares and longings stored
boldly before God's gracious throne,
where you will have a lasting home.
Don't view events through worldly eyes,
but fix your focus on the skies.
For Christ, triumphant, will return
to banish pain and calm concern,
all evil schemes to overwrite,
reverse the curse and set things right.

SEX *Holding Up Plan A*

God has a sexual order that lets human beings flourish. When you break that pattern, everything goes crazy.

— Pastor David Engelhardt

READ: 1 Cor. 7:1–13, 1 Thess. 4:1–8, Heb. 13:4

Like a Virgin

In 1987, I asked my parents for Madonna's *Like a Virgin* cassette for my birthday. As strict Evangelicals, they promptly declined. After all, her songs don't encourage remaining a virgin long. Madonna is a feisty boundary-pusher who authored a steamy coffee table book in 1992. In it, she proudly flaunted her sexual "freedom." You might be shocked to learn that married Christians following biblical guidelines can have better sex than Madonna.

Her storied life involves flitting from one man or woman to the next, aborting a child, and divorcing twice. It smacks of botched intimacy. At age sixty-seven, failed attempts to erase her age have rendered her almost unrecognizable.

No Botox Needed

Conversely, for Christians, wrinkles and gray hair should not keep spouses from being attracted to one another. Unlike most celebrities, Christians don't fear rejection due to physical disabilities, age, or appearance. The stability of such relationships enables spouses to focus on what matters most to God.

Guardrails

"Many societal problems wouldn't exist if everyone followed God's design for sex," Kay Faust said in an interview with Becket Cook. "Pretty much every social ill is overpopulated by the same demographic: fatherless children." She mentioned that the fatherless account for 90 percent of homeless teens, 63 percent of teens who commit suicide, and 71 percent of teen pregnancies.[10]

While far from perfect, most Christians take biblical guidelines on sex seriously. They save physical intimacy for marriage and consider it a permanent covenant before God. Disciples of Christ know that God designed sex to permanently bond people. That's why when a sexually active couple splits, it feels like ripping two glued individuals apart. No one escapes unscathed.

Whether single or married, we need to know the truth about sex to apply it ourselves and mentor others. Some characterize God as a buzzkill when it comes to this delicate topic. But He invented sex and called it good. He made men and women complementary. He set up guardrails so intimacy could be most fully enjoyed. God wrote the manual on how relationships function best. Here are some guidelines Christians agree with. Sex is best when

- both parties feel loved, accepted, and safe
- the participants are married to one another (not committing adultery or hooking up)
- both parties trust one another and are unselfish
- no one fears pregnancy or sexually transmitted diseases
- it bonds people who are committed to staying together

APPLICATION

1. Under what circumstances does God permit sex? Why did He design it this way?

2. Are you embarrassed to discuss sex? God isn't. It's important to share age-appropriate biblical truth with the next generation. It will save them a lot of heartache. Who in your life needs to hear this?

3. If married, have you withheld sex to get back at your spouse? If so, reread 1 Corinthians 7. If unmarried, what does 1 Thessalonians 4:1–8 say you should prioritize? If you struggle with lust, find a faithful Christian to hold you accountable.

FURTHER READING: *Holy Sexuality and the Gospel* **(2018) by Christopher Yuan**

SONG: "Arise My Love" (1990) by Michael Card

ONE

Whispers of hazy purple sunset
hang like smoke over distant mesas.
Under cool desert darkness flows the brook:
evenly, quietly...content...
over waiting stones, to clear pools below,
calm and steady, tracing smooth, familiar channels
worn by decades of connection.

PEOPLE PLEASING *Roots and Solutions*

I was so concerned with what people thought. And, you know, whether it was my upbringing or my woundedness along the way that really got its hook in me. . . . it was connected to the fear of rejection.

— Tasha Layton

READ: Prov. 29:25, Gal. 1:6–11, 1 Thess. 2:3–8

Rejection

Louise's father abandoned his ten children before she could read. One fateful day, he told them that he was leaving to marry someone else. That instant, Louise became an ardent people-pleaser. She scanned every face to assess their approval or disapproval of her. What she dreaded most was another loved one abandoning her. She obeyed her mother, cared for her younger siblings, and put herself last . . . for decades.

Roots

On the surface, people pleasing doesn't seem like a serious issue. People-pleasers are, by definition, kind and accommodating. They're afraid people will abandon them if they don't keep them happy. Therefore, they say yes to every request. For them, "being needed" ranks as a top priority. People-pleasers are often unaware of the deep-seated motivations driving their choices.

Low self-esteem is a hallmark of people-pleasers. These beleaguered individuals base their self-worth on their performance. Louise *needs* to be needed. She *needs* to be thanked and then thanked again for gifts or acts of service.

Side Effects

This sentiment bleeds into our spiritual lives, tainting our relationship with God. We begin to feel like He's only pleased with us when we're accomplishing things. We think we must earn God's grace. Since God sees us through the lens of Christ's perfection, we are righteous. Nothing can make God love us less. Parents can attest to how they love their children unconditionally.

Fallout

It's frustrating. Everyone loves Louise, but everything she does comes with strings attached. Any gift or act of service demands excessive thanks. Unfortunately, seeking approval from others usually ends in disappointment. Louise's "love tank" is not *only* always empty. It has a *hole* in the bottom that no amount of validation can patch. This causes her to feel unloved and makes her hypersensitive to what she deems criticism.

Solutions

When we're exhibiting people-pleasing tendencies, we must rethink our motives to get back on track. One way to begin is learning to say no nicely and *only* volunteering for activities we feel called to do. When asked to sign up for something that doesn't fit for us, a response of "I'm not currently available" should suffice. There's no need to apologize or make excuses. We don't have to feel guilty for maintaining healthy boundaries and prioritizing what matters.

Dozens of worthy causes compete for our time and attention. But God doesn't intend for us to meet everyone's needs. While it may seem innocuous, people pleasing weakens relationships, diminishing our margins and placing the approval of *others* above that of God. We will only rediscover our voice and know our value when we realign our thinking about approval.

APPLICATION

1. Do you have a hard time saying no when asked to do something good? If so, why?
2. How much do you care about the approval of others on a scale from one to ten? Memorize Galatians 1:10. Seek God's approval above all else and listen to what He says to prioritize.
3. Do you need to free yourself from activities you signed up for? What do you feel led to cut in order to focus on your purpose?

FURTHER READING: *Boundaries: When to Say Yes, When to Say No to Take Control of Your Life* (1992) by Henry Cloud and John Townsend

SONG: "Godpleaser" (1983) by Petra

HEEL

He runs back and forth along the fence
barking at people of whom he's unsure.
He frantically dives deep in the pool,
doggy paddles his heart out,
and leaps back into the yard.
He doesn't know how to heel.

She runs back and forth around the room,
trying to sound so sure of herself.
She always dives in with both feet
to rescue hopeless cases she calls friends.
She leaps into helping, longing for validation.
She doesn't know how to heal.

CREATION *Implications of Intelligent Design*

The more I study nature, the more I stand amazed at the work of the Creator.

— Louis Pasteur

READ: Eccl. 3:11, Jer. 32:17, Rom. 1:20, Col. 1:16

Creation Teaches Us

My biology teacher taught the theory of evolution. Over billions of years, by chance, the universe and everyone in it allegedly materialized. Humans are just animals, evolution tells us.

Romans 1 tells a different story with far-reaching implications. From the beginning of time, people have instinctively known there was a Creator. God has made His attributes known through Creation. Creation teaches us that God is powerful, artistic, beautiful, playful, detail-oriented, mathematical, constant, mysterious, colorful, and vast. The duck-billed platypus demonstrates that God has a sense of humor.

The evidence for intelligent design has existed since Genesis: an organized, complex world. Astronomer Fred Hoyle said that if we see a Boeing 747, we don't assume a tornado went through a junkyard. We assume intelligent beings designed and built it. Isaac Newton, a master physicist and astronomer said, "Atheism is so senseless. When I look at the solar system, I see the earth at the right distance from the sun to receive the proper amounts of heat and light. This did not happen by chance."

Creation Referenced as Real

Scholars have identified 103 allusions to the Genesis account in the New Testament alone. **Even the Bible's final book (Revelation 4:11) emphasizes that God is worthy to be praised because He created all things.** Therefore, if the Creation account is a fairytale, so is a large percentage of the Bible. You can't have it both ways.

Morality Hinges on God

If we're evolved animals, why is killing someone wrong? Why is *anything* wrong? Does the cheetah feel remorse for killing its prey? Animals don't share our sense of morality. We're not evolved animals. If we were, puppies would be as valuable as humans. However, God created us in His image so we intuitively know right from wrong. In His perfection, God sets all moral standards. He personally oversaw our development in utero and loves us as only a parent can.

APPLICATION

1. Have you been taught the theory of evolution as a fact? Even Darwin admitted that the human eye is far too complex to have evolved. How can you initiate a discussion about Creation with others?

2. What aspects of Creation best support intelligent design?

3. If everyone has proof of a Creator, why are there so many atheists? How have people you know "traded the truth of God for a lie"? This week, examine your beliefs and make sure they're in line with God's Word.

FURTHER READING: *The Lie: Unraveling the Myth: Evolution/Millions of Years* (2024) **Ken Ham**

SONG: "Evolution . . . Redefined" (1993) by Geoff Moore & The Distance

---

MY LIGHT AND GUIDING STAR

Adonai is my Light and Guiding Star.
He flung suns into space and planets afar.
The orb He created burns hot at noon.
To watch over night, He hung the full moon.
He Who Sustains knows each nova by name
and sprinkles the heavens with comets aflame.
Even swift lightning bolts from His grasp.
Borrowing brilliance, the dawn shall advance.
Our bright Morning Star leads our pilgrimage home,
where each traveler is loved, each wayfarer known.

CHARITY *How Helpless Feels*

You can see churches that are attempting to manifest themselves as neighbors rather than saviors. . . . who understand that the guiding Christian principle is friendship, not service.

— John McKnight

READ: Isa. 41:10, Matt. 25:34–40, James 1:27

The Receiving End

Growing up, I was frequently on the receiving end of charity. As the youngest of three, most of my clothing was hand-me-downs. I didn't realize the financial disparity between me and my peers until middle school. My wealthier peers would take trips to some unknown paradise called "Florida" and ski in Colorado. Was I jealous? Maybe just a little.

The Giving Side

Fast-forward forty years. I've been married to a generous Christian for thirty years. Raised by his grandparents as an only child, my husband didn't experience financial struggles growing up. Thankfully, in the last decade, I've often found myself on the *giving* side of charity rather than the *receiving* side.

I work as a missionary translator. The best part of my job is traveling the world, visiting children at sponsorship sites and putting on English camps. But I didn't really understand the feelings of those we help until recently.

"Free" Flights

In January, my flight attendant brother gave me free flights anywhere American Airlines flies directly to or from the U.S. However, I must fly standby. So if a flight is full, I don't get on.

In July, I visited sponsorship sites in Brazil. I wanted to fly from Chicago to São Paulo, saving $3,000. But the flight was full. Eventually, I made my way through New York to São Paulo. That wasn't too bad. But *escaping* Brazil proved to be quite a challenge.

I planned to fly from São Paulo to Miami on July 14, arriving home July 15. Weather issues canceled most flights from São Paulo to the U.S. Consequently, the remaining flights overflowed with paying passengers who had been bumped. I never stood a chance. I spent Monday night in São Paulo. The next day, naïve and bushy tailed, I returned to the airport, assuming I'd get home. But instead of arriving on Tuesday morning, I arrived home *Friday* morning. I was stuck in Brazil for three days and in Miami for two days.

By the end, I was so frustrated, I couldn't keep myself from sobbing openly in the airport. I couldn't understand why my prayers were seemingly hitting a brick ceiling. From my limited perspective, it felt like God wasn't taking care of me. Like I'd requested bread and gotten a stone.

How It Feels

When I returned from Brazil, I pondered what the trip taught me. Then it hit me. The needy families we serve feel helpless and frustrated like I did. They likely feel that God doesn't care about them, even though they know He does. I imagine they hate their lack of agency over life outcomes. What a terrible emotional space to live in!

I lost hope when I realized there was nothing I could do to improve my situation. I was at the mercy of circumstances beyond my control, and praying didn't seem to help.

How to Help

How can we help those we serve avoid this trap of despondency? We can **ask them to help us** as they're able. For me, this involved asking Brazilians to pray for a difficult family situation I'm facing. Their sincere prayers proved to be powerful and effective. *My* need enabled them to give something *to me*. After years of receiving charity, I'm sure it feels good to be in a position to give it.

We can also **guide those we serve through an asset-based thought process**. Ministries should consider their strengths, weaknesses, and assets. We can help people identify and mobilize resources they already possess. This approach empowers people.

Finally, we can **treat those we serve as peers**. We can stay in contact with them and treat them as equals within the body of Christ. Colonial hierarchies have no place in the Church. Every part of the body of Christ is essential and should be valued.

In his groundbreaking book *When Helping Hurts*, Steve Corbett says that poor people who aren't from North America describe their condition using words like shame, inferiority, powerlessness, and humiliation. In contrast, he says that North Americans emphasize a lack of material things. The less fortunate don't need our stuff. They need us to understand how helpless feels.

APPLICATION

1. Have you ever felt embarrassed or helpless when receiving charity? How did you feel and why?
2. How can you provide help to those in need without encouraging dependency or making them feel less-than?
3. Do you treat missionaries or people from less wealthy countries differently than your neighbors? Ask the Holy Spirit to convict you if so. Ask an international friend to pray for something that's on your heart.

FURTHER READING: *When Helping Hurts: How to Alleviate Poverty Without Hurting the Poor . . . and Yourself* **(2004) by Steve Corbett and Brian Fikkert**

SONG: "Hands and Feet" (1999) by Audio Adrenaline

FROM EVERY NATION

Brown hand holds black hand holds white hand holds beige.
Interconnected, we mirror his face.
Bound by compassion, entwined in His grace,
never constrained by time, race, or place.
Holding our Bibles high over our heads,
with manna from heaven, our spirits are fed,
following our Shepherd wherever we're led.
For *all* Jesus died, for the nations He bled.
No matter the oceans, or jungles, or plains;
we stand united in Christ's holy name.
Watching and waiting till one day we reign,
thriving forever without fear or pain.

HUMILITY *I Must Decrease*

The stamp of the Saint is that he can waive his own rights and obey the Lord Jesus.

— C. S. Lewis

READ: Isa. 66:1–4, Mic. 6:1–8, James 4:1–12

"Next week, we're starting a sermon series on humility," your pastor announces. You don't audibly sigh, but you think to yourself, *Boring.* You've been a Christian for decades and don't feel you need another lecture on humility.

Recently, a lady from church spoke about this topic. Instead of drafting a speech, she printed out twenty applicable Bible passages. We read them aloud, then discussed how they applied to our lives. This made me think of practical ways that even mature Christians can increase in humility.

Acknowledge Who's in Control (Hint: It's Not You)

Sometimes I feel that if I want something done right, I have to do it myself. When I travel for work, it seems nothing gets accomplished in my absence. But how arrogant is it to believe that the world will fall apart if I don't control every situation? Do we really think that if we take a break, God can't handle things without us?

Recently, beloved pastor and author John MacArthur passed away. Shortly before that, someone asked him how his ministry could continue in his absence. He wisely responded that if you put your hand in a bucket of water and take it out, water fills the empty space. He humbly explained that he was not indispensable.

Place Yourself Under God's Word

In our culture, many assume that if their opinion differs from what the Bible says, *they're right*. We must avoid this grave error. "Why wouldn't God bless the union of two people who love each other?" some might protest. Well, I've never found any verses encouraging homosexuality. Instead of planting pride flags in churchyards, let's have the humility to submit to God, asking him to illuminate passages we don't understand. If we disagree with God on doctrine, guess who's right?

Think of Others

Another hallmark of humility is taking a genuine interest in others. C. S. Lewis famously wrote, "Humility is not thinking *less* of yourself; it is thinking of yourself *less*." Americans often focus on how life isn't fair. We dwell on how the sinful actions of others negatively impact us, but we don't often see these people through God's eyes or admit our own contributions to problems.

What We Deserve

Anyone familiar with the Bible knows that we *do not want* to get what we deserve. What do we "deserve"? An eternity in torment away from everyone and everything we love. We don't want God to be fair. We want him to be merciful.

This week, take the *U* (you) out of humility and put others back in. Rest and listen, letting God be God. Submit to God's Word. Above all, remember that without God's intervention, not one of us would glimpse heaven.

APPLICATION

1. How can you grow in humility this week?
2. God opposes the proud and gives the humble grace. What are the negative consequences of being proud? Do you want God to oppose you? Ask the Holy Spirit to convict you of pride in your life.
3. List any Bible passages you don't understand. Discuss them with a doctrinally sound, mature believer, and resolve to obey God's revealed will.

FURTHER READING: *The Blessing of Humility: Walk Within Your Calling* (2016) by Jerry Bridges

SONG: "The Basin and the Towel" (1994) by Michael Card

WHO IS LIKE THE LORD OUR GOD?
(an original hymn)

His voice sustains the oceans, spanning endless skies.
His might moves massive mountains. His mind needs no advice.
The fount of life and wisdom, His plans we cannot grasp.
Stars are set aflame by Him; His hand we cannot clasp.

CHORUS
Who is like the Lord our God, conquering our vicious foes?
Building kingdoms, tearing down. His mind none can know.
Who is like the Lord our God, Shelter from the pelting rain?
Echoes of his kindness still and heal all our pain.

All the world's nations are teardrops in the sea,
sapling plants, so fragile, frail . . . so soon our spirits flee!
We feel our burdens are ignored or that our God cares not.
Providence is on His throne. Our feeble frames forgot.

All the world runs after decaying grass and wood.
Clamoring for finer things, we have not understood.
Our Father fashions futures and never falls asleep.
He reigns above our destiny. His hand our lives will keep.

Machinations of His plans can't cross our weakened minds.
But when we faint, He strengthens us to cross the finish line.
We'll win the treasure kept for us, weighty golden crowns,
and live forever with our Lord . . . at His feet we'll bow.

TRIALS *Walk Through Deep Waters*

Ultimately the only answer God gave to Job was a revelation of Himself. . . . Job was not asked to trust a plan but a person, a personal God who is sovereign, wise, and good. It was as if God said to Job: "Learn who I am. When you know me, you know enough to handle anything."

— R. C. Sproul

READ: Ps. 69:1–29, Isa. 43:1–2, Daniel 3

Once, during a mission trip to Haiti, our truck needed to cross a river without a bridge. We stopped at the water's edge. Men waded in to measure its depth. They knew our truck could be destroyed driving through deep waters. They deemed the crossing safe and our pickup forded the river.

Isaiah 43:2 promises that God is with us when we're out of our depth in "deep waters." Perhaps you've experienced a looming diagnosis, sudden loss, or painful relationship. These events plunge us into racing rapids that threaten to carry us away. But when inevitable trials crop up, God holds our hand and walks with us.

Similarly, in Daniel 3, three friends whose Hebrew names were Hananiah, Mishael, and Azariah faced certain death when bound and thrown into a furnace. It was so hot, the soldiers who threw them in died. But God showed up and didn't leave these three faithful servants alone in their ordeal. "A fourth man" walked in the fire with them. Many believe this fourth man was the preincarnate Christ.

Psalm 69 is an imprecatory song that pleads with God for help. David seeks divine intervention as floods overwhelm him. He asks to be plucked from the mire and drowning waves. He recalls God's mercy and might. The psalm ends on a positive note: Those who love God will dwell in safety.

Next time we feel overwhelmed by tragedy, let's reframe our chaos and focus on this truth: God is not apathetic. He will hold and sustain each of us until our life's work is done.

APPLICATION

1. List any tragic experiences that overwhelmed you.
2. Does God leave us to our own devices when we're in trouble? Record how God helped you through a crisis.
3. How can you remind yourself or someone else that as God's children we never suffer alone? Which Bible verses could you memorize?

FURTHER READING: *Streams in the Desert* **(1925) by L. B. Cowman**

SONG: "Let the Waters Rise (2009) by MIKESCHAIR

WALK THROUGH THE FURNACE

Walk through the furnace, firestorms blazing.
Wade through deep waters, for I am there too.
Ford flowing rivers, fighting strong currents.
I swear you won't drown, for I'll see you through.
I know your new name; I wrote your story.
I have a purpose that's tailored to you.
I'll carve a pathway through sandstorms and centuries.
I know you're weary; your strength I'll renew.
Boldly you're facing brazen oppression.
Lift heads to heaven; I'm coming for you.
Face your bright future, leaving past wonders.
They can't compare with what I've planned to do.
I'll lead you home soon, one sunny morning;
you'll understand my grand plan for your life.
Faithfulness echoes, pulses through memories,
banishing sorrow and ceasing all strife.
Here there is only blessed abundance;
every past problem has vanished like mist.
Colors that quiver, joy you can't fathom,
ages of sunshine and unceasing bliss.

TAKING ACTION *Be an Abigail*

From her humble position, Abigail saved her husband, all their servants, and all their belongings. And because her heart was right before her evil husband, God honored her for the cruelty and abuse she'd endured for so many years and positioned her to become the wife of a soon-to-be king.

— Denise Renner

READ: 1 Sam. 25, Est. 5:1–8, Esther 7

Dad always called me a woman of action, like Abigail, due to my tendency to act quickly in emergencies. In college, I was always the first person out of the dorm when the fire alarm rang. As an adult, when I see an urgent need, I do my best to ensure it gets met.

At age six, my niece was diagnosed with brain cancer. She and her family were missionaries in Spain. I prayed that God would heal her but also researched her cancer. Unsure whether the Spanish doctors had selected the ideal treatment, I consulted an oncologist at church. He informed me that a nearby hospital reviews pediatric cancer records weekly. I got them to assess her records for free to ensure the best treatment.

When crises arise, we should always begin with prayer. We should be empathetic and kind. But there are times when the most godly thing we can do is take action. Nabal's wife, Abigail, illustrates this through her quick thinking.

Nabal was a rich but bad-tempered man. His wife, Abigail, was discerning and beautiful. It was sheep-shearing time, and David's men had protected Nabal's workers and herds in the fields. As was customary, David's men politely requested food from Nabal, who rudely refused. Offended, David swore to kill every male in the household. Although she didn't cause the problem, Abigail learned of the situation and sprang into action. She had food prepared and rushed it to David and his men.

Though she was of high standing, Abigail humbled herself, bowing at David's feet. She apologized on behalf of her foolish husband. She demonstrated faith in God and appealed to David's conscience. Shrewdly, she framed the situation to show how God had saved David from senseless violence. David realized that Abigail's actions had averted bloodshed. He blessed her and told her to go in peace. (And later married her, but that's a different story.)

Instead of exhibiting fear or anger in this unfair situation, Abigail took charge and made things right. While we always want to empathize with problems, often the best response includes promptly taking action, like supplying food or shelter. Abigail saved many in her household that day.

APPLICATION

1. What practical actions can you take that would be helpful in the difficult situations you or others are facing?
2. Which of your relationships would benefit from a dose of selflessness? Abigail's humility paved the way for a positive outcome. If necessary, apologize to someone this week.
3. From our other reading, what are some things Esther did to save her people?

FURTHER READING: *Crazy Love: Overwhelmed by a Relentless God* **(2013) by Francis Chan**

SONG: "Do Something" (2012) by Matthew West

ABIGAIL

A wealthy man named Nabal had a lovely wife.
His churlish, boorish attitude ruined her whole life.
For years she waited, held her tongue, submitted to the Lord.
She sought to serve her Master earning heavenly rewards.
The manager of servants, she ran her house with care.
Everyone respected her and blessed her in their prayers.
One day, providence arrived in the form of soldiers.
Nabal's arrogance had caused David's ire to smolder.
Bent on killing everyone in Nabal's noble house,
David and his fighters raced to kill her cruel spouse.
Abigail heard this threat and quickly sprang to action.
With food and drink she humbly aimed to placate warring factions.
On her knees with great respect, she begged the future king
to keep himself from bloodshed, to step back from war's brink.
Astonished, captivated, David smiled and thanked the Lord
for this lovely woman who saved many from the sword.
Many years of drinking had hardened her old mate.
Many years of patience finally brought a better fate.
Once the Lord struck Nabal down, Abigail was free.
Her wisdom and her actions brought justice and relief.

GENEROSITY *A Godly Response to Mercy*

Any fear associated with giving to God's kingdom is irrational. It's on par with a farmer who, out of fear of losing his seed, refuses to plant his fields.

— Andy Stanley

READ: Deut. 14:22–29, Phil. 4:10–20, 1 John 3:17

100 Percent?

My husband had just earned his real estate license. Although he worked as a programmer, he wanted to do a few real estate deals for extra income. A few months later, I jumped for joy when he informed me his client was purchasing a small apartment building. The commission would weigh in at a hefty $10,000. He then told me he had promised to give God 100 percent of his first commission check. "Are you sure you said 100 percent?" I asked, hoping he'd opt for a tithe. My husband's spiritual gift is giving, so we ended up donating $10K to charity. There's a well somewhere in Africa because of my husband's generous heart.

Two Perspectives

I didn't grow up learning generosity. Although my parents were believers, they both came from disadvantaged families. Penny pinching came naturally to them. Due to our financial situation, I had to pay for half of my college tuition. I worked at school and held down summer jobs to pay down this bill. When I needed a car, Dad sold me one for $2,000 . . . and added it to my mounting tab.

Conversely, on his sixteenth birthday, my husband's grandparents handed him the keys to a new Mustang. We married one year after college graduation. I still owed my parents money for the car. I felt embarrassed when my husband's family paid off my debt. I knew my parents loved me, but at times it felt like they cared more about getting repaid. Some of my friends keep tabs on "who owes who what." If I pay for lunch, they think they owe me that money. Since I've been living with a generous man for a while, I've learned that true love never keeps track. Not of money, not of service, not of wrongs.

Financial Fears

It's natural to cling to money when we're afraid we won't have what we need. When the Philippian church donated, Paul assured them that God would supply all their needs. As Charles Spurgeon said, "God has a way of giving by the cartloads to those who give away by shovelfuls." We cannot outgive God. The song "Slow Me Down" succinctly describes this sentiment: "When my grasping hands are afraid You won't provide, will You . . . set your table here with what truly satisfies?"[11]

Whose Money?

Christian businessman, R. G. LeTourneau, once said, "It is not how much of my money I give to God, but how much of God's money I keep for myself." All wealth belongs to God and should be used to further his Kingdom. If we steward well what God temporarily entrusts to us and His generosity can flow *through* us, He'll entrust us with more. In Luke 12:34, Jesus said that our hearts will be wherever our treasure is. First John 3:17 says that God's love isn't present in those who, seeing a believer in need, refuse to help. When Christians find themselves in dire straits, donating to them benefits both the giver and the recipient. Someday in heaven, our joy will be complete when we discover what God did with the loaves and fishes of our offerings.

APPLICATION

1. Loving relationships are never characterized by withholding. God lavished grace on us at an unfathomable expense. How can you become more godly in your giving?
2. What's your attitude toward paying for things? Do you have a cheapskate mentality? What if God acted like this toward you?
3. What do you think of the following Amy Carmichael quote: "You can give without loving. But you cannot love without giving"?

FURTHER READING: *Fields of Gold* (2004) by Andy Stanley

SONG: "My Worth Is Not in What I Own" (2014) by Keith and Kristyn Getty

THE ECONOMY OF GOD

Humble yourself; be lifted up.
Lose in life; gain in death.
Serve subordinates; reveal leadership.
Put yourself last; be first in the Kingdom.
Give from the heart; get more than you need.
Serve in secret now; be richly rewarded later.
Be a pilgrim on Earth; be a citizen in Paradise.
Walk by faith here; walk by sight there.
Know little now; know all things then.
Lose your life to truly find it.

PERSECUTION *The World Isn't Worthy of Them*

In a country where Christians were looked upon with suspicion and disfavor, a government leader said to me with a twinkle in his eye, "Christians seem to thrive under persecution. Perhaps we should prosper them, and then they would disappear."

— Billy Graham

READ: 2 Thess. 1:3–12, 2 Tim. 3:10–12, Heb. 11:32–40

The Gathering

Muslim background believers, also known as "MBBs." I first heard this term in 2019 prior to a mission trip to the southern Philippines. It denotes brothers and sisters in Christ who grew up Muslim and then converted. While the majority of Filipinos are Catholic, most inhabitants of Mindanao, next to Indonesia, are Muslims.

Culturally Muslim, these brave souls have given their lives to Christ and been shunned by their communities. In Mindanao, those who convert from Islam to Christianity receive death threats. ISIS frequently kidnaps people and forces young men to fight for them. Often, Christians there aren't allowed to sing at church services. Instead, they take to the Sulu Sea in boats. Far offshore, they worship the Lord in song safely.

Once a year, these downtrodden MBBs gather together in Christ. In 2019, I witnessed a thousand precious persecuted believers come together to fellowship. They performed cultural dances, offered regional products as offerings to God, and encouraged one another in the faith. At one point in this service, a former Muslim cleric asked anyone who had been tortured or persecuted for Christ that year to stand up. My jaw hit the floor as several people rose from their seats. My mind raced to Hebrews 11. The world isn't worthy of them.

Anti-Christian Policies

I've never been persecuted anywhere close to what these people have experienced. I'm not even worthy to tie their shoes. India recently passed legislation prohibiting charitable donations from other countries like the US. This has hamstrung ministry there. In addition, states like Uttar Pradesh in the north have anti-conversion laws, making it a crime to convert from Hinduism to Christianity.

Attention Fence-Sitters

In the US, we have long had the dubious privilege of being able to sit on the proverbial religious fence. However, the assassination of Christian conservative apologist, Charlie Kirk, on September 10, 2025 has forced many to admit where they stand ideologically. When asked what the 31-year-old wanted his legacy to be, he said, "I want to be remembered for courage for my faith."

We may never experience the level of persecution of our international friends. Or perhaps last week's murder of a staunch evangelical for promoting biblical truth indicates that we might.

Whatever happens, be strong in the Lord and in his mighty power this week. May we never be ashamed of the gospel. As Ericka Kirk posted from Psalm 46 hours before her husband drew his last breath, "God is our refuge and strength, an ever-present help in times of trouble." So we *will not fear* even if the mountains plunge into the heart of the sea.

APPLICATION

1. Have you ever experienced persecution because of your faith? Describe it.
2. How can you honor, bless, and support persecuted Christians this week? Visit the Voice of the Martyrs website.
3. Would you have the strength to stand for Christ, even if it meant losing your family, job, or life? Ask God to enable you to stand firm for your convictions.

FURTHER READING: The Cost of Discipleship (1937) by Dietrich Bonhoffer
SONG: "Over My Dead Body" (1984) by Steve Taylor

NO TURNING BACK

Sulu Seas roll through in crests,
outcome fixed, no turning now.
Signed away life's dying breath,
to idols knee shall never bow.
Lacking family, now I'm dead,
clinging only onto You.
Past life sinks with water's ebb;
Paradise, my hopes accrue.
I shall stand, intrepid, brave.
They may kill this mortal tent;
though my path snakes to the grave,
my soul awaits its swift ascent.

SILENCE AND SOLITUDE *Come Away*

*Retire from the world each day to some private spot... Stay
in the secret place till the surrounding noises begin to fade out
of your heart and a sense of God's presence envelops you....
Listen for the inward Voice until you learn to recognize it....
Gaze on Christ with the eyes of your soul.*

— A. W. Tozer

READ: Mark 1:32–36, 6:30–32, Ps. 131

"Quiet time." That Christianese word that we use. Is your soul, you
mind, your body quiet? I'm a raging extrovert, but even I require
stretches of silent solitude to replenish my soul and organize my
chaos. Jesus hung out with His disciples or crowds most of the time.
He knew He needed to get away from the noise to hear His Father's
heart and stay the course.

Why Bother?

If Jesus did it, we should too. How can pulling away from modern life
for a time benefit us? Isolating ourselves from our hectic schedules
helps us **hear God's voice better**. For example, Elijah went up to
Mount Horeb to hear God, and Habakkuk stood alone, keeping
watch and waiting for God to speak. The apostle Paul spent years in
Arabia prior to his ministry to be alone with God.

This spiritual discipline also **breaks our addiction to noise and hurry**. Author Donald S. Whitney believes that the "convenience of sound" (having music, TV, videos available 24/7) has contributed to the spiritual shallowness of contemporary Christianity. We are rarely alone with our thoughts and God's voice. I live in the Chicago suburbs. Even when hiking in a forest preserve, if I stop, I can hear not only the rustling leaves but cars, planes, and lawn mowers. True silence eludes me. However, when I visited a twelfth-century French village at five a.m., the contrast punched me in the face. On the cobblestone path, surrounded by irises, jasmine, and roses, I paused, breathing in the misty air. I perked up my ears. The song of a distant lark, the wind through the grass and . . . nothing. I froze like a rabbit trying to hide. Inconceivable. Not a single air conditioner, conversation, or vehicle broke the morning air.

"There's no better way to step back and get a more balanced, less worldly perspective . . . than through silence and solitude," writes Whitney in *Spiritual Disciplines for the Christian Life*.[12] In addition, such times help us *discern God's will*. Even Jesus spent time alone with God before choosing who would be His disciples.

How Can I . . . ?

Plan ahead for an extended time of silence and solitude. Find a quiet place, like a library, park, or church. Schedule a minimum of two hours. Bring along a Bible, a journal, and whatever Christian books you want to read. If you can't find that much time, get up thirty minutes before anyone else and use that time.

Over the years, I've accumulated a variety of journal questions for my "retreats":

- What's making me feel anxious?
- What do I control about that situation?

- Which relationships should I invest more energy into?
- What's one thing I can do to improve my physical or mental health?
- What has God been teaching me lately?

APPLICATION

1. Have you been able to hear God's voice lately? If not, make sure to find a quiet place and listen. Write down what He says.

2. What percentage of your waking hours are you listening to music (or other noise)? Why?

3. What questions would you like God to answer? Put your next "retreat" on the calendar.

FURTHER READING: *Spiritual Disciplines for the Christian Life* **(1991) by Donald S. Whitney**

SONG: "In Stillness and Simplicity" (1988) by Michael Card

SWEPT

Entranced by fields and countryside
at dawn, I tread medieval streets.
To ancient stone, small ferns cling tight.
White jasmine blooms infuse the breeze.

To hear the drone of background noise,
I pause my steps; I perk my ears.
Save warbling birds in rustling firs,
in rising sun, the air is clear.

No single car, or plane, or train
disrupts the fragile balance there.
No mowing motors, humming sounds,
nor voices slit the dewy air.

From sweetest silence how to tear
my newly quiet, heart appeased?
My mind swept clean by mistral winds
resets my anxious soul at ease.

WEEK 44

YOUR NEW NAME *Becoming*

There is an identity you have in God, reflected in your new name, that transcends whatever shame or regret or disappointment is wrapped up in who you are now. There is a very private and personal place of intimacy with him that brings hope and freedom and joy that none can touch or taint or steal away.

— Sam Storms

READ: Gen. 17:1–8, John 1:42, Rev. 2:17

What's in a Name?

In Old Testament times, name changes signified new beginnings. God called Abram to leave everything he knew and journey to a vast, uncharted wilderness. God vowed to raise up a great nation from this childless old man's descendants. To mark the occasion, God gave the ninety-nine-year-old a new name, Abraham, which means "exalted father."

Simon, son of Jonah, was a hotheaded fisherman. Simon means "one who hears." Simon's life consisted of searching for fish. One day, his world was upended. He laid down his nets to fish for souls instead. Seeing in Simon something imperceptible to others, Jesus boldly renamed him Cephus, or Peter, which means "rock." Christ gave him a new name to reflect his new identity in God's family.

Koustsostamatis to Axelson

My name should be Mrs. Koutsostamatis (Κουτσοσταματις) instead of Mrs. Axelson. When his mom had him in 1973, my husband's original name was Georgos Knute Koutsostamatis. His biological father ensured his firstborn got baptized in the Greek Orthodox church. His mother secretly had him baptized at the Swedish Covenant Church without her Greek husband's knowledge.

Before his third birthday, Georgos lost his Thessalonian dad in a bitter divorce. In retrospect, it was a blessing that my husband's biological father did not raise him. The man refused to pay thirty dollars a month to visit his young son. In fact, in the divorce settlement, Georgos's dad cared most about preventing anyone from changing his son's Greek name. Georgos's maternal grandfather, Nils Axelson, and his lawyers agreed to this stipulation. "We accept this restriction, but you can never contact your son again." "Fine," replied the twenty-four-year-old with a northern Greek accent, "but his name stays Greek," he affirmed with a twinge of sorrow and national pride.

With his mother's blue eyes and his father's dark hair, Georgos straps on his kindergarten backpack. Grandma Lois Axelson walks him to school and signs him up as "Knute Axelson." "Knute" isn't his first name. "Axelson" isn't his last name. But it's 1978, and no one bats an eyelash.

Knute's mother soon remarries, and at age six, he opts to permanently live with his grandparents. Though he would later discover five half-siblings, Knute is raised as an only child. Knute doesn't remember his father and would no longer recognize him.

He doesn't need to either. Knute knows who he is. He wears his Swedish heritage proudly and considers his grandparents his parents. In spite of his real name, everyone in high school calls him Knute Axelson.

When the SAT exams roll round, they take attendance. "Koutsu . . . Koutso-stam-atis? Is there someone named Georgos here?" Knute slowly raises his hand, sensing a spotlight on his introversion. His peers scoff. His name is so long, no one can pronounce it. What's this guy's actual name? Who are his parents? Behind their questions hides the desire to know who Knute's people are—to whom he belongs.

Despite the divorce agreement, Knute could change his *own* name after turning eighteen. The day after Christmas in 1991, Georgos Knute Koutsostamatis stands before a judge to petition for a legal name change to "Knute Gustaf Axelson." He's allowed to change his first, middle, *and* last name. "Knute" has always been his middle name. "Axelson" is his mother's maiden name. But "Gustaf" . . . why choose Gustaf as a middle name?

Karl Gustaf Axelson, later known as Grandpa Gust, left his home in Sweden in September 1916 at age nineteen. He braved the ocean to travel to America. He arrived under the torch in New York Harbor, as if it were beckoning him to create his legacy—something wild and beautiful, beyond his dreams. His son, Nils Gustaf Axelson, would become the administrator of the Swedish Covenant Hospital in Chicago and serve in the U.S. Navy in World War II. These are Knute's ancestors—his past, his present, and somehow his future.

At age eighteen, Knute pays homage to them by selecting "Gustaf" as his middle name. He honors his grandparents by taking their last name. In 2003, he names his only son Soren Gustaf Axelson. Regardless of biology, Knute *knows* who his family is, to whom he belongs. In this context, he's free to become who God created him to be.

Knute also has a home in God's family. As a believer, he has no questions about his identity. No longer an only child, he's blessed with millions of brothers and sisters and citizenship in heaven. At the end of time, Knute will get a new name that only God knows to carry him into eternity.

APPLICATION

1. What do you think of your name? Who gave it to you? Does it have any significance? What do you think your new name will entail?

2. Look up Bible passages about name changes like Jacob to Israel, Naomi to Mara, or Sarai to Sarah. What do the new names indicate?

3. Thank God for how well He knows you and for your membership in His family.

FURTHER READING: *Heaven: A Comprehensive Guide to Everything the Bible Says About Our* **Eternal Home (2004) by Randy Alcorn**

SONG: "Deep Enough to Dream" (1997) by Chris Rice

I'M

I'm on the precipice of who I'm meant to be.
I'm on the edge of what I'm meant to do.
I'm on the brink of self-actualization.
I'm on the verge of bursting with potential.
I'm on the threshold of stepping into my new name.

MEDIA CONSUMPTION *Garbage In, Garbage Out*

Where we cast our gaze, and for how long, influences not just how we live but who we are.

— Jen Wilkin

READ: Ps. 101:1–4, Luke 11:33–36, Eph. 4:25–32

Fancy Trash

Our sixth-grade teacher walked into Bible class. The graying, no-nonsense teacher dumped out a bag onto her desk. On a glass plate, she placed garbage. A banana peel, candy wrappers, tissues, tin cans. Piling it high, she pulled out a can of whipped cream. Like a professional, she swirled a large dollop atop the mess. She then added sprinkles, chocolate syrup, and a cherry. We sat silent, mystified.

Many girls in our class had been reading "Christian" fiction books about young prostitutes. Each book chronicled the conversion of a working girl. But most read it for the sensational details about the seedy underworld. Miss Bingham sternly announced, "Garbage is still garbage . . . even if you dress it up with whipped cream and a cherry."

Options

This "fancy trash" object lesson was forty years ago, yet the point remains valid. Christians might not struggle much with the temptation to read inappropriate books anymore given our easy access to online and streaming content. Nowadays, we can secretly watch any garbage we want in the privacy of our homes. The options are endless. How are modern Christians to sort through the mess if they watch anything at all?

The Missionary

We love hosting our friend who runs a seminary in India. One evening, as my husband and I settled in to relax after work, it hit us. Could we watch our normal shows if the missionary watched *with* us? Unfortunately, we've often compromised "because a show is so good" and welcomed steamy scenes, obscenities, and violence into our home. Our missionary friend appeared. We played it safe and settled on "Forged in Fire." Realty shows about blacksmithing rarely offend.

Then I thought about which shows I'd have to nix if Jesus were sitting next to me. A long list. Then it dawned on me. Jesus is always watching with me. I felt convicted about certain shows and removed them from my watch list. It's just not worth it.

David's Advice

Psalm 101 says we shouldn't look with approval on anything that is vile. We should have nothing to do with perversion. David learned the hard way (by his sinful choices) that what we choose to look at influences our actions and our hearts.

The words we hear influence us as well. Many moons ago, I watched the movie *JFK* at home. I figured I could fast-forward anything objectionable. Wrong. The entire film is laced with obscenities. My mind was so full of them, even I had a hard time not dropping F bombs for the next twenty-four hours. Learn from my mistake. It's better to miss a film or show than to fill the temple of the Holy Spirit with garbage.

Broadcasting the Hidden

You can't unhear or unsee things. Pornography and darkness sneak into our homes, marring all that's sacred. One day, the Bible says, all that's hidden will be announced to the world. Would you watch everything you watch if it would be broadcast at church on Sunday? Ungodly content only hurts you and your family. Hidden sin eats away at our souls. But it can't survive exposure. Admission thrusts shameful habits into the light where they can be destroyed.

Setting the Bar

I'm so proud of our young adult son. He has stringent standards for what he watches. If he walks in and sees a couple is kissing on TV, he groans and exits the room. He's actively fleeing youthful lust. This will serve him well as he progresses in his spiritual life and one day leads a family.

WWJW? What would Jesus watch?

APPLICATION

1. Are there unsavory images stuck in your head because of what you've watched? Confess that sin and ask God to erase that memory. Fill your mind with what is good, true, and beautiful.

2. Would you be embarrassed to have everything you watch be broadcast? If so, nix the shows that would embarrass you.

3. Is the Holy Spirit prompting you to stop watching certain content or shows? Tell a Christian friend and set up guardrails to keep yourself from accessing it. Err on the side of purity.

FURTHER READING: *The Common Rule: Habits of Purpose for an Age of Distraction* **(2019) by Justin Whitmel Earley**

SONG: "People in a Box" (1985) by Farrell and Farrell

WWJW?

What would Jesus watch?
What would Jesus skip?
Would the *Desperate Housewives*
have Him in their grip?
Would severed heads and violence
flood His TV screen?
Would horror films and gore
fill His home with screams?
Would leftists on *The View*
be spilling gossip tea?
Would talking heads be mocking God?
Would He vote for me?
Gay men kissing gay men
and steamy, sexy scenes.
Would He watch hot dancers
or proud transvestite queens?
Would He crave a bigger home?
A built-in retro bar?
Would He buy a castle
or a million-dollar car?
Would F bombs bomb His Netflix feed
or surgeries now botched?
How would Jesus spend His time?
What would Jesus watch?

CULTIVATING GRATITUDE *0.5 World Problems*

You say, 'If I had a little more, I should be very satisfied.' You make a mistake. If you are not content with what you have, you would not be satisfied if it were doubled.

— Charles H. Spurgeon

READ: Num. 11:1–34, Col. 3:15–17, 1 Tim. 6:6–10

Although it's no longer politically correct to categorize problems as "third world" or "first world," this week's devotional discusses what I call "0.5 world problems." The Bible instructs us to give thanks in all circumstances, but it's easy to grumble when things don't go our way. Focusing on our miniscule problems can lead to lacking perspective and gratitude. Instead of being concerned about where our next meal is coming from, we might become enraged if our favorite Starbucks is closed for remodeling. It's a sad state of affairs when Christians grumble about "first world" problems.

However, it's even worse to complain about what I dub "0.5 world problems." Here's a list of real-world, yet unimportant, things people have complained about. I'm not pointing any fingers here. I've had to step back from selfishly worrying about minute details of my life to gain a more godly perspective. Have you ever groused about any of the following?

- Your kitchen lacks sufficient counter space for your toaster, bread maker, blender, stand mixer, food processor, panini press, Instant Pot, and waffle maker.
- Your existing bathroom faucet is brushed nickel, and brass is trending now.
- Your three cars don't fit in the driveway.
- The battery died on your cat's indoor drinking fountain. (True story!)
- Your rental SUV doesn't have a heated steering wheel.
- You can't remember the combo to your fireproof safe.
- You can't fit a double-wide Sub-Zero refrigerator in your proposed kitchen renovation.

It's reminiscent of the children of Israel complaining after God rescued them from slavery. I can hear them now. "I sure would like a good leek and cucumber sandwich. I'm so sick of quail and manna."

Recently, I told a group of kids about the global child sponsorship program I work for. Its aim is to break the cycle of poverty and share the gospel. In an effort to put things into perspective, I had the kids raise their hands if 1) they'd had more than one meal that day, 2) they get to go to the doctor when necessary, and 3) they have the privilege of attending school. The next day during homeschooling, one of these children said, "Mom, I don't want to do spelling, but I know there are other kids in the world who are saying, 'I want to do spelling!'"

APPLICATION

1. Write a list of "0.5 world" problems that aggravate you. Then, rewrite your list with an attitude of gratitude. Turn each problem into something to be grateful for. For example, "I wish I could renovate our bathroom" becomes "I'm thankful to have indoor plumbing."
2. Have you let inconveniences steal your joy? If so, confess your ungrateful attitude. Each day this week, write down four things for which you're grateful.
3. List all the abilities, assets, good relationships, experiences, etc. God has given you. Take inventory of your blessings frequently and thank God for them.

FURTHER READING: *One Thousand Gifts: A Dare to Live Fully Right Where You Are* (2011) **by Ann Voskamp**

SONG: "Thankful Heart" (1986) by Petra

A MODERN PSALM 100

Lift joyful hearts in thankful songs.
Our God is good and all day long
He keeps us safe in His embrace
with perfect love, enduring grace.
We are His flock; He meets our needs.
We follow where our Shepherd leads.
We thank our Lord, for He provides
sun and shelter, moon and tides.
Unfailing love guards all our ways.
We enter our King's courts with praise.
His faithfulness is our salvation;
it will reach each generation.

TRUSTING GOD *Even When Panicked*

Jesus isn't worried about the future. Don't live in the past or the future (what will happen if...). God has provided me with everything I need to live in this moment.

— Katie Davis Majors

READ: Isa. 46:3–11, Jer. 17:5–8, Luke 1:5–23

As a middle school teacher, I chaperoned a yearly camping trip. To encourage team building, everyone had to navigate the high ropes course. I'm not afraid of heights. I *do* have a healthy fear of falling two stories on my head, though.

As I climbed up the rickety ladder, I felt the tall pines shifting in the wind. Once harnessed, I was supposed to cross the abyss balancing on a rope and reach the next platform. Initially, my adrenaline and anxiety kicked in, like when you lean too far over a high railing. But I couldn't wimp out because I wanted to set a good example. I eased onto the highest rope and inched along. Then, I lost my balance and fell three feet until the harness caught me. After that, I was fearless. The worst-case scenario was I'd waste a few seconds getting back on the course after the harness saved me. You know where I'm going with this. Often, it's only after we "fall off the rope" of life and find God's arms there to catch us that we begin to trust Him.

In Luke 1:13, Gabriel tells Zechariah that he'll have a son in his old age. The second Zechariah questions God's revelation, he can't speak. The angel explains in verse 20, "Every word I've spoken to you will come true on time—*God's* time." (The Message) This has always been true. Yet I'm quick to open my doubting mouth like poor Zechariah. When panicked, I try to remember God's sovereignty and faithfulness.

The Object of Our Trust

As Tim Keller says, "If you're falling off a cliff, strong faith in a weak branch is fatally inferior to weak faith in a strong branch. Salvation is not finally based on the strength of your faith, but on the object of your faith." When we face crises, we must remember that we aren't trusting in our own strength but in God's.

Read the End of the Book

In our high school youth group, we had monthly student sharing times. One time, my friend Dave simply pointed to Revelation and said, "Read the end of the book. We win." Our light and momentary troubles are achieving for us a glory that far outweighs them. We must remember that, like the Shane and Shane song "You've Already Won" proclaims, we're fighting a battle that God has already won.

Resurrection Power

I saw a video of Dr. Tim Keller recorded in 2020 (before his death in 2023) in which he said that if Christ was really resurrected, everything's going to be okay. He added that we don't know *how* it's going to be okay, but it is. We serve a trustworthy God who raises the dead.

My Redeemer Is Faithful

There's an old Steven Curtis Chapman song that always bolsters my faith. He talks about being back on the road he's traveled and seeing the many times God carried him through that his Redeemer is faithful and true.[13] Can't we all testify that when the rubber meets the road, God always comes through? I didn't say He'd let us know ahead of time exactly what will happen, as I'd prefer. In my experience, He's rarely early and never late.

In his song "Firm Foundation," Cody Carnes describes how he has built his life on Jesus and how Jesus has never let him down. He asks the question "So why would He fail now? *He won't*" (emphasis mine).[14]

APPLICATION

1. When have you been scared and trusted God? Did He fail you?
2. When discouraged, read the last two chapters of the Bible. We win. What truths can you learn from these chapters?
3. Do you agree that God is rarely early and never late? Give an example. How can you prove you're trusting God this week?

FURTHER READING: *You Can Trust God to Write Your Story* (2019) by Nancy DeMoss Wolgemuth and Robert Wolgemuth

SONG: "My Redeemer Is Faithful and True" (1987) by Steven Curtis Chapman

---

THE WORLD'S IN YOUR HANDS

(inspired by the Spanish portion of Evan Craft and Danny Gokey's song "Everything Will Be Alright")

Father, I confess with an open heart
that I'm lost in this desert of false starts.
The chinks in my chain mail have been exposed.
My car seems very far from your chosen road.
Why does the sun no longer dawn on my days?
Why are my nights so cold, far from your gaze?
Why do I feel like something is lacking?
Why does this gray road feel like it's cracking?
I know You're at work even when I don't feel it.
I know You're at work even when I don't see it.
I know I will escape this wretched maze.
I know I'll win this fight and give You praise.
I know that these floods will one day recede.
I know that in You, my plans will succeed.
I know that even though I can't understand,
I take comfort in knowing that the world's in your hands.

THE UNSAVED *What to Expect*

The key word for us is not debate; it's dialogue. It's having a friendship with someone who may be far from God where we create a safe place, where they're willing to express their doubts and their questions and their skepticism.

— Lee Strobel

READ: Rom. 8:5–17, 1 Cor. 3:1–10, 2 Cor. 4:1–6

What Do You Expect?

A friend of mine was complaining that her unsaved husband was watching racy videos. While I agreed this was unacceptable, I also reminded her that he wasn't a Christian. She constantly nagged him to be a better man: to go to church, to help around the house, to be a better dad. This made the problem worse. Her husband didn't have a new nature. He didn't have the Holy Spirit convicting him and helping him. I suggested that she concentrate on her own spiritual growth and pray for her husband. Although she'd married a non-Christian, she expected him to act like a believer. This frustrated everyone. Even Christians can't go twenty-four hours without sinning, so let's not be too hard on our unsaved friends. The good news is that he came to Christ a year later.

Debate vs. Dialogue

Our InterVarsity leader, Mark Ashton, was a great apologist. But even *he* said we can't argue people into the Kingdom. Some people enjoy arguing and wouldn't believe even if God showed up in person. Very few people reject Christ due to honest intellectual doubts.

That's why we should share Christ within the context of loving relationships, telling others what God has done in our lives. It's hard to argue with someone's testimony of transformation.

The Results Are In

We're in charge of obeying God and sharing the gospel, but remember, God is in charge of the results. First Corinthians 3 tells us that some plant gospel seeds while others water them. Some harvest. But *only God* can make seeds grow. It's okay if we aren't the ones leading people to Christ right and left. As my youth pastor Rich says, "My goal each day is to nudge each person I see closer to Christ." Just nudge.

Give Me Your Eyes

Jesus saw the lost as "sheep without a shepherd" and wept for them. God created each of our unsaved loved ones and has a purpose for each life. He loves each individual enough to die for them. I've found it helpful to see people through this lens.

How does God see them? Many people put on a brave face while falling apart inside. They strive to gain money, power, and prestige. Once they have it, they realize it doesn't satisfy. They're afraid of dying. They want their children to flourish, but the advice our culture gives them is harmful.

A prayer of mine, as the Brandon Heath song, "Give Me Your Eyes" says, is, "Give me your heart for the ones forgotten. Give me Your eyes so I can see."[15]

APPLICATION

1. Do you see people as valuable? God does. Ask God to give you His love for someone you are struggling to love.

2. Instead of insisting that non-Christians behave like the regenerated, expect that they'll act enslaved to their sinful nature. That the gospel is veiled to their eyes. Pray for them. Nudge them toward Christ.

3. Have you treated annoying people as Christ would? Confess any ways in which you haven't viewed others through His eyes.

FURTHER READING: *Out of the Saltshaker and Into the World: Evangelism as a Way of Life* (1979) **by Rebecca Pippert**

SONG: "Part of Your Story" (1997) by Cheri Keaggy

FIRE AND ICE

Icy tears sting grief-stained face,
but deep within, God's warmth and grace
threads through my throbbing soul.
Racing through vermillion veins,
icicles of hatred melt
on fires of forgiving hearts.
Uncontrollable, I weep.
My triumphant smile mocks
the tyrants: fear and pain.
Guillotine gales wind-whip hair,
I feel them not—for Christ's truth sears
holes throughout my selfish mind.
His mercy and compassion
can illuminate the darkness
in a forsaken, frozen world.

VISION *Calling Out Gifting*

A vision we give to others of who and what they could become has power when it echoes what the spirit has already spoken into their souls.

— Larry Crabb

READ: 2 Tim. 1:3–11, Titus 2:1–8, 1 Pet. 5:1–4

Potential Pastor

After becoming a Christian, Canadian pastor Toe-Blake Roy didn't know what to do in life. A church elder noticed that he excelled at public speaking. The elder invited him to preach at a small country church, and Toe-Blake did. When he graduated high school, this more mature Christian encouraged him to go to Bible school. He saw the potential pastor this young man could become. God did the rest.

Casting Vision

Titus 2 indicates that more mature believers ought to be setting an example for younger people and encouraging them to reach their God-given potential. Sometimes, that involves casting a godly vision for what they can become.

When God called Gideon from hiding in a winepress to leading an army, Gideon couldn't see this future for himself. The angel greeted Gideon, calling him a mighty warrior. Like Moses, Gideon thought God had chosen the wrong person for the job.

When did someone first believe in you and encourage you to pursue your purpose? For me, it was when my parents paid for a student trip to France they couldn't afford. I wanted to major in French, and they sacrificed to make that dream a reality. My French teacher also noticed my potential. In high school, she let me teach French to beginners. I've been a French teacher, translator, and missionary since college.

Check Your Gifting

Pastor Rick Warren created a useful acronym to help people discover their "SHAPE" in ministry. Filling out this inventory guides Christians as to where they can best use their gifting.

S – spiritual gifts
H – heart (what they're passionate about)
A – abilities
P – personality
E – experiences (positive and negative)

As Gary Chapman wrote, "Each person has the potential of making a positive impact on the world. It all depends on what you do with what you have." May God clarify his vision for us and those around us this week.

APPLICATION

1. Fill out the SHAPE inventory for yourself. Make plans to guide someone else to use this tool.
2. Make a list of adults who helped you become who you are today. If possible, thank them.
3. List any younger individuals in whom you recognize gifting. Ask God how you can help them fulfill their purpose.

FURTHER READING: *The Purpose Driven Life: Why on Earth Am I Here?* **(2002) by Rick Warren**

SONG: "Who God Is Gonna Use" (1991) by Rich Mullins

LEGACY

I jolted awake
after fifty lethargic years.
I had sleepwalked through life
far too long,
relegating dreams to the domain of darkness,
lacking the courage to free them from their chimerical corral.
But when midnight struck on the morn of five decades,
I began liberating dormant poetry, passions, and projects.
Possibilities pranced from their paddock
into the wilderness of potential.
Pintos, chestnuts, dapples, grays,
appaloosas, roans, and bays
parading proudly
past my mind's eye
into the light of legacy.

HEAVENLY REWARDS *Sending Treasures Ahead*

In that day, the full truth about their lives, character, and deeds will be made clear to each believer. Each will discover the real verdict on his or her ministry, service, and motives. All hypocrisy and pretense will be stripped away; all temporal matters with no eternal significance will vanish like wood, hay, and stubble, and only what is to be rewarded as eternally valuable will be left.

— John MacArthur

READ: Matt. 6:1–8, 1 Cor. 3:10–15, 2 Cor. 5:6–10

When I was twelve, I heard about doing good deeds in secret at Sunday school. I didn't want to lose my reward from God by being praised by people. So I snuck into the kitchen and began loading the dishwasher. When my parents walked in on me "secretly" doing good, I felt disappointed. "Now I'm not going to be rewarded in heaven," I sighed.

Henry Parsons Crowell, the philanthropist who owned Quaker Oats said, "Every man is a fool who gets rich on earth but not in heaven." He donated over 70 percent of his wealth to charities like the Moody Bible Institute in Chicago.

How It Works

How do rewards in heaven work? Second Corinthians 5:10 says that even Christians will be given what they deserve for the good or evil they have done. This doesn't mean that we'll be eternally condemned for sins we've committed. Romans makes it clear that there's no condemnation for believers. In addition, 1 Corinthians 3:11–15 says Christians will be rewarded for their good deeds. It explains that unimportant or sinful things they've done will be "burned up."

The Bible says we'll receive back from God whatever good we do. Therefore, we should make it a priority to figure out what God will reward. In this way, we can send treasures ahead to heaven where they can never be taken from us. Here's an inexhaustive list of what God says He'll reward in heaven:

- Suffering/bearing insults for Christ
- Praying and fasting in secret
- Generous giving
- Loving our enemies/doing good to them
- Showing hospitality to those who cannot repay it
- Demonstrating compassion for the vulnerable, hungry, sick, homeless, imprisoned, poor
- Doing quality work
- Enduring pressures in ministry
- Keeping the faith through trials
- Doing good and being loyal to God and His family
- Obeying God's laws
- Seeking holiness, justice, righteousness

We all know that coffins don't have storage and that whoever dies with the most toys doesn't "win." In the time that remains, we should fill heavenly coffers with treasures that will last. May we always be searching for ways to please the Lord, stewarding the time, money, and abilities He has given us well.

APPLICATION

1. How good are you at fixing your eyes on unseen things? What can you do this week to remind yourself that this life isn't as important as eternity?
2. Choose three of the things God rewards and commit to doing them this week.
3. Do an anonymous act of kindness this week. It's amazing how fulfilling this is. I would give you examples of what I've done, but then I wouldn't be rewarded in heaven, so . . .

FURTHER READING: *A Life God Rewards: Why Everything You Do Today Matters Forever* **(2002) by Bruce Wilkinson**

SONG: "Thank You" (1988) by Ray Boltz

THE LIFE GOD REWARDS

Christ will appear in wonder one day
with angels at His side.
Then He'll repay each person for
the way they lived their lives.

Some people build with precious stones,
while others gild with gold.
Some construct with straw or wood
that dies, decays, and molds.

Don't let possessions possess your mind
or captivate your soul.
For where your greatest treasure lies,
your heart and hope will follow.

Send riches ahead to a place
where rust cannot destroy.
There, victories of our lifelong race,
rewards we will enjoy.

Don't seek praise or trumpet good
as hypocrites love to do.
But serve in sacred secrecy.
The Father will reward you.

May you fight the good fight,
persevering in the faith.
May you always yearn for the Groom's return,
preparing as you wait.

HEAVEN *One Foot Over the Jordan*

How you think about Heaven affects everything in life—how you prioritize love, how willing you are to sacrifice for the long term, how you view suffering, what you fear or don't fear.

— John Burke

READ: 1 Cor. 15:35–58, 2 Cor. 5:1–10, Rev. 21

I stood at the front of the church, greeting droves of people who turned out for Dad's funeral. My feet hurt and my makeup was smeared by tissues. A former theology student of Dad's gave me one piece of advice. Read Randy Alcorn's giant book *Heaven*. In the weeks that followed, I purchased the book. Now that I had a cherished relative "on the other side," a newfound interest in the afterlife had sprung up. Alcorn's book began with biblical truths we often skip.

Our loved ones who have died in Christ don't yet have resurrection bodies. All believers, the Bible says, will be given new bodies at the same time, like waiting for everyone to wake up before opening Christmas gifts. That means there's an "intermediate" heaven, when those who are absent from the body are present with God.

One day, God will create a new heaven and a new earth. There, in a world untainted by sin, we will spend eternity without physical limitations. We will feel nothing but God's pure love and the joy of serving Him.

Another book that has informed my view of heaven is *Imagine Heaven*. In it, John Burke reveals the results of over a hundred interviews of individuals who had near-death experiences. All the accounts corroborated the biblical narrative. People reported feeling an overwhelming sense of being loved, enhanced senses of sight, sound, etc., and being able to communicate and travel effortlessly.

What will eternal life be like in the new heaven and new earth God will create?

What's There

    God, angels, worshippers
    Believers from every century and culture
    Trees with fruit, rivers of life
    Celebration, feasting
    Love, belonging
    Satisfying work, reigning

What's Not

    Temptation, sin
    Worry, sadness
    Pain, limitations
    Frustrations, aimlessness

N. T. Wright says, "So far from sitting on clouds playing harps, as people often imagine, the redeemed people of God in the new world will be the agents of his love going out in new ways, to accomplish new creative tasks, to celebrate and extend the glory of his love."

APPLICATION

1. Do you have loved ones who are with the Lord? Does that make you want to know more about heaven? What are two things you learned about heaven?
2. Did you know that no one has their resurrection bodies yet? What will our new bodies be like?
3. In heaven, people feel an overwhelming sense of unconditional love and belonging. How can you create an environment like that now to welcome people?

FURTHER READING: *Imagine Heaven: Near-Death Experiences, God's Promises, and the Exhilarating Future That Awaits You* (2015) by John Burke

SONG: "Finally Home" (2007) by MercyMe

DIMLY AS THROUGH A GLASS

I see now as through darkened glass.
On this side, nothing's clear to me.
The other side eludes me still,
and hid behind the glass, glory.
Angels long to pierce the veil,
just to glimpse His perfect plan.
A pilgrim here, I know too well
how short my meager life will span.
Windows straddling heaven and earth,
have finally been opened wide,
as I traverse this unclear path,
bathed in blessings at His side.
When I arrive in Zion's sun
with all my trials laid to rest,
I'll know as I am known by Him,
my tapestry unfolded, blessed.

LEGACY *What Matters Most*

The greatest legacy one can pass on to one's children and grandchildren is not money or other material things accumulated in one's life, but rather a legacy of character and faith.

— Billy Graham

READ: Ps. 78:4, Ps. 112:1–3, Prov. 20:7

In 2023, I turned fifty. Instead of getting a new car or husband, I took a writing class. I've been writing poetry since fourth grade. Most is saccharine drivel about unicorns and dreams. However, the class inspired me to compose new work and get it published. How can those of us who no longer qualify as "spring chickens" leave a lasting legacy?

As in life, games are won or lost in the second half. Regardless of missteps and missed opportunities in the first half of my life, I resolved to make a difference. Passing down stories, photographs, and traditions ensures our stories don't end with us. Focusing our efforts on what we excel at and are passionate about also helps us leave our mark. Here are three actions to take to flourish in this season of life.

Capturing Stories

First, chronicle your family history before everyone who remembers it is gone. I recently unearthed an essay my grandmother wrote. In riveting detail, she recounted a true story about driving a pair of horses that ran away with her. (If you're curious, she bailed out and the horses sprinted back to the barn.) She noted how she met my grandfather and described her love for adventure. It won't win any awards, and most people have no interest in these stories, but my family loved them.

In addition, consider putting together a physical or digital scrapbook of family memories. Every year on their birthdays, I drag out my children's baby books. It keeps them grounded and reminds them they have always been loved. I don't have time to photo-document every event, but I always make Christmas scrapbooks. Each year, we smile to see old holiday photos of our loved ones who are no longer with us.

The Bible makes it clear that we should share stories of God's faithfulness with the next generation. Joshua 4:21–24 says, "Then Joshua said to the Israelites, 'In the future your children will ask, "What do these stones mean?" Then you can tell them, "This is where the Israelites crossed the Jordan on dry ground." . . . He did this so all the nations of the earth might know that the LORD's hand is powerful, and so you might fear the LORD your God forever.'" As Joshua did after crossing the swollen Jordan River on dry land, set up your own stones of remembrance by recounting all the times God carried you through life's raging waters (Joshua 4:4–7).

Passing on Traditions

One meaningful tradition my parents began was taking each of us individually on mission trips. My mom has always loved other cultures and faraway lands, and we've always attended churches with strong missions programs. As a Bible professor, Dad had a heart for cross-cultural ministry. He loved the Jordan Groom quote, "If God calls you to be a missionary, don't stoop to be a king." He passed away eight years before I became a missionary, but I think he knows and is happy.

Every morning, tucked in his den, Dad would pray for the 30-50 missionaries whose prayer cards plastered the walls. Most of them had been his students at Moody Bible Institute. Given this background, it will come as no surprise that our parents deemed it important to take each of us on a mission trip to the Caribbean. My mom took me to Jamaica when I was in sixth grade. Before you start daydreaming of Montego Bay, I will specify that we served Jamaican missionaries in the bustling capital of Kingston.

You don't have to take your kids on mission trips, but research shows that volunteering increases mental health in teens. Find a local charity or a ministry at church and involve your whole family in serving. Your example of service will resonate through the generations that follow.

Following Our Gifting

The last way to leave our mark on future generations is to discover our gifting and passion and begin focusing on them. What subject makes your eyes light up with excitement when you discuss it? What do you excel at? What activities make you feel fulfilled?

For me, it is speaking French, scrapbooking, traveling, and teaching. I'm blessed that my husband has a "real" job that covers our costs. This has enabled me to blossom and reach my full potential.

APPLICATION

1. What unique gifts has God given you? I'm a realtor, but millions of people have successfully bought and sold homes. I long to focus on things only I can do, like translating sacred French poetry into English and making it rhyme or creating a poem to sing for every Psalm in the Bible. What is it that *only you* can do?

2. Grab a cup of coffee or tea and find somewhere quiet. Break out a journal or digital note and brainstorm how you can use your history, hobbies, and gifts to make your life count.

3. Bring to mind one time God did something important for you. Perhaps He guided you to your spouse or your career. Maybe He made the impossible happen. Tell this testimony of God's greatness to someone this week.

FURTHER READING: *Becoming Sage: Cultivating Meaning, Purpose, and Spirituality in Midlife* (2020) by Michelle Van Loon

SONG: "Legacy" (2002) by Nichole Nordeman

TWELVE STONES IN THE RIVER
(based on Joshua 3-4)

These thousands of pilgrims, so weary, so spent,
believe in their hearts that their destiny lies
to the west of this mighty, unfordable river,
whose raging banks swell like blood-livid eyes.
With bated breath, Jericho's walls wait to fall.
The priests of the Lord with the Ark of His promise
march boldly to reach their rival's broad shores.
Closing their eyes, they pray to survive; sandals stay dry.
Torrents snake to the sea. Walls of water grow doors.
Thousands of travelers cross it, amazed.
Twelve tribes take twelve stones from Jordan's dark floor.
Joshua piles twelve stones more in the center.
On sinewy shoulders, boulders are borne
to their home on the plains of mighty Gilgal,
a striking reminder to children's children.
These twelve special stones mean the God of the cosmos,
no talisman, statue, nor jinn, nor idol,
against hopeless odds led his people right here,
through a bloated, swift-flowing, perilous hurdle,
to fields of milky and honey-kissed gifts.
We still see stones standing, staunch in the river.
Their miraculous story cries out to be told.
For those who step out on the shore of God's will
unimagined and marvelous power unfolds,
forever inspiring a legacy of faith.

ACKNOWLEDGEMENTS

The paths of the Lord throughout my life have proven inscrutably wonderful and beyond comprehension. I never dreamed I would have the privilege of writing a book. In the end, fulfilling our purpose in life comes down to listening to those who have affirmed our gifting and believed in us—who caught hold of the vision God planned for us long ago.

Pastor Greg Norwine is one such person. Greg served as the pastor to young adults when my husband, Knute, and I were dating in 1995. In 2004, I joined Greg and others on a mission trip to the Congo, which, in turn, sparked the creation of the EFCA's child sponsorship program, GlobalFingerprints. Sixteen years later, in 2020, Greg asked me to consider applying for a job with GlobalFingerprints, and I soon became a missionary translator. The EFCA encourages its missionaries to improve their communication skills for ministry partnership development. Therefore, in 2023, at age fifty, I took the "Write Your Life Lessons" writing class with Diane McDougall. I learned that God has given me a story to tell and a way to describe it that resonates with others. Thanks to Jeff Hill and other Christian authors, I began to shed my imposter syndrome and lean into storytelling.

My husband, Knute, has played (and continues to play) a vital role in my blossoming into a Christian writer and becoming the woman God created me to be. Undaunted by little promise of compensation, Knute has always loyally stood by my side, encouraging me to flourish in my gifting and calling. I can never thank him enough for his calm companionship, wisdom, and love.

In 1998, Knute and I began attending the Arlington Heights Evangelical Free Church in Illinois because we enjoyed the sermons of its new pastor from Scotland, Colin Smith. Growing up in the church, I had heard thousands of sermons since I first trusted Christ in 1978. But Pastor Colin's sermons renewed my love for biblical exposition. The way he wove together overarching biblical story lines with obscure Old and New Testament references enthralled me. Over the decades, I have taken copious sermon notes and incorporated many of Colin's teaching themes into my spiritual journey.

Over five decades, the snowball of life lessons and tragedies has eventually brought me to a rich place of being able to teach and comfort others with what God has taught me. Countless conferences, Christian books, and conversations have provided fodder for a year's worth of life lessons. My mom, Carol Ashby Nevin, has always been my biggest cheerleader and for that I am thankful. My dad, Dr. Paul Nevin, always loved mining the riches of God's Word, teaching, and writing. Now, I am thrilled to pick up the torch of his dream.

NOTES

1   "The Super Bowl Shuffle," written by Bobby Daniels, Lloyd Barry, and Melvin Owens, produced by Richard E. Meyer, Red Label Records, 1985.

2   Corrie ten Boom, excerpt from *The Hiding Place, 35th Anniversary Ed.* (Chosen, 2006), 247–48, in "Guideposts Classics: Corrie ten Boom on Forgiveness," Guideposts.com, https://ca.thegospelcoalition.org/article/the-forgiveness-of-corrie-ten-boom/.

3   Julia Ubbenga, *Declutter Your Heart and Your Home: How a Minimalist Life Yields Maximum Joy* (Zondervan, 2025), xv.

4   "Slow Me Down," performed by Porter's Gate, written by Jon Guerra Sandra McCracken, Integrated Music Rights, 2023.

5   "In Christ Alone," by Keith and Kristyn Getty, written by Keith Getty and Stuart Townsend, produced by John Schreiner, 2006.

6   Robert McGee, *The Search for Significance* (Rapha Publishing, 1985), 40.

7   Andy Crouch, *The Life We're Looking For: Reclaiming Relationship in a Technological World* (Convergent Books, 2022), 14–17.

8   Edith Schaeffer, *The Hidden Art of Homemaking: Creative Ideas for Enriching Everyday Life* (Tyndale House, 1985), 202.

9   Henri Nouwen, *Reaching Out: The Three Movements of the Spiritual Life* (Image, 2013).

10 "A Warning to Us All: Katy Faust Interview – The Becket Cook Show," episode 208, July 31, 2005, https://www.youtube.com/watch?v=wICoJ4iizz8.

11 "Slow Me Down," performed by The Porter's Gate, featuring Jon Guerra and Sandra McCracken, written by Kate Bluett, Leslie

Jordan, Matthew Kaemingk, Sandra McCracken, and Wendell Kimbrough, produced by Isaac Wardell, 2023.

12 Donald S. Whitney, *Spiritual Disciplines for the Christian Life* (NavPress, 2014).

13 "My Redeemer Is Faithful and True," performed by Steven Curtis Chapman, written by Steven Curtis Chapman and James Isaac Elliott, produced by Steven Curtis Chapman and Brent Milligan, 1987.

14 "Firm Foundation (He Won't)," performed by Cody Carnes, written by Cody Carnes, Austin Luke Kaleolanakila Davis, and Chandler Moore, produced by Austin Davis, 2023.

15 "Give Me Your Eyes," performed by Brandon Heath, written by Brandon Heath and Jason Ingram, produced by Dan Muckala, 2008.

ABOUT THE AUTHOR

JOY NEVIN AXELSON grew up in West Chicago, Illinois, and attended Wheaton Christian Grammar School and West Chicago High School. Her father, Dr. Paul Nevin, taught theology and hermeneutics at Moody Bible Institute in Chicago for thirty-two years. Her mother, Carol Nevin, is a marriage and family counselor. She lives near Joy in Northbrook at Covenant Living.

Joy came to Christ at age five and was baptized at the West Chicago Bible Church at age sixteen. She studied French at the University of Illinois (Champaign-Urbana) and at the University of California (Santa Barbara) in hopes of serving as a missionary in France.

God had other plans. In 1994, after returning from studying abroad in Strasbourg, France, Joy met Knute Axelson at InterVarsity. They wed at the Northbrook Covenant Church in 1996. They share two young adult children, Soren and Linnea.

In 2021, Joy began serving as a part-time missionary with the Evangelical Free Church of America's child sponsorship branch, GlobalFingerprints. She works as a translation coordinator,

ESL teacher, and care worker trainer. To learn more, visit https://joy-axelson.mailchimpsites.com.

Joy wrote her first poem in fourth grade (circa 1983) and continued authoring mostly saccharine poetry about unicorns and sunsets throughout middle and high school. In 2023, at age fifty, Joy took a Christian writing class and began chronicling her crazy stories and life lessons.

Joy hopes to have her devotionals translated into several languages and to publish many more books. Her next project, titled *52* More *Life Lessons I Learned the Stupid Way*, should be available late next year. For now, those wishing to have her free weekly devotional emailed to them can sign up at her website (www. JoyNevinAxelson.weebly.com).

Joy hopes you enjoyed (no pun intended) her book. Feel free to reach out to her on Facebook or at JoyNevinAxelson@gmail.com.

www.ingramcontent.com/pod-product-compliance
Lightning Source LLC
Chambersburg PA
CBHW020232130626
46549CB00005B/1857